EVERYDAY COOKING

From novice to chef step-by-step recipes

Everyday Cooking
Published in 2009 by Hinkler Books Pty Ltd
45–55 Fairchild Street
Heatherton VIC 3202 Australia
www.hinklerbooks.com

Cover design: Imagine Graphic Design
Internal design: Hinkler Books Studio
Typesetter: Midlands Typesetting
Pre-press: Graphic Print Group

2 4 6 8 10 9 7 5 3
10 12 14 13 11

Disclaimer: The nutritional information listed under each recipe does not include the nutritional content of garnishes or any accompaniments not listed in specific quantities in the ingredient list. The nutritional information for each recipe is an estimate only, and may vary depending on the brand of ingredient used and due to natural biological variations in the composition of natural foods such as meat, fish, fruit and vegetables. The nutritional information was calculated using Foodworks dietary analysis software (Version 3, Xyris Software Pty Ltd, Highgate Hill, Queensland, Australia) based on the Australian food composition tables and food manufacturer's data. Where not specified, ingredients are always analysed as average or medium, not small or large.

ISBN: 978 1 7418 2602 9

Printed and bound in China

Contents

Introduction v

Conversions vii

Starters 1

Pasta, Rice & Noodles 27

Sides 49

Vegetables 75

Chicken & Seafood 99

Meat 125

Desserts & Sweet Treats 149

Index 173

Introduction

Keep *Everyday Cooking* handy and you'll never be fazed again by what to make or to take! With its repertoire of great recipes – easy enough for everyday, elegant enough for entertaining – this cookbook is sure to become a staple of your kitchen. Among the uncomplicated but irresistible ideas you'll find good things to satisfy all tastes and cater to any number, from a couple to a family group to a bigger gathering.

Choose from savoury, sweet, hot, cold and warm dishes of lively tastes and textures as centrepieces or support acts. The selection ranges from the familiar (enlivened with a twist) to the more unusual or the deliciously different, drawn from a number of cuisines and cultures. Recipes are straightforward and speedy to prepare, and combine mostly everyday ingredients. When slightly more exotic ingredients are called for, these should be easy to obtain and inexpensive. And if you are looking to serve something particularly suited to the weather or a method of cooking (for example, on the barbecue or in a wok) you'll find it here too.

Clear step-by-step written instructions and photos demonstrate how to prepare and present your choices. Large photos of the finished product show exactly what it is you are making and provide some serving or presentation ideas. For each recipe, useful information on preparation and cooking times, as well as the nutritional value (fat, carbohydrate and protein) of each serving, is given.

The seven sections of *Everyday Cooking* are organised to make menu planning simple. Each section is comprised either of recipes based on a particular kind of food – chicken, seafood, meat, rice/pasta/noodles, vegetables – or the kind of dish – a starter, soup, side or dessert. By mixing and matching between sections, you'll be able to put together tempting spreads that deliciously fit the bill from morning to night!

The seven sections

The individual sections listed below show how *Everyday Cooking* can work for you, whether you are an accomplished or a not-so-experienced cook.

1 Starters

These tasty starters play all kinds of roles, depending on the occasion, how many to be fed, the time you have or the effort you want to go to. There are soups ranging from the light and delicate to the definitely hearty; flavoursome, bite-sized serves of chicken, meat and seafood; and more-ish finger food and titbits. Serve them as appetisers, snacks, part of a brunch or light lunch, a supper or for passing around at a party.

2 Pasta, rice and noodles

The versatility of pasta, rice and noodles is amazing. In some cases, you can use them interchangeably in recipes, giving you even more options for delicious results. In the selection provided, these staples are combined with meat, chicken, seafood, vegetables or eggs for meals with real zing. Turn out risottos, pilafs, curries, casseroles, salads, soups, stir-fries and pasta and noodle dishes from the East and West – you won't believe it's so easy to impress!

3 Sides

Well-chosen sides can turn a main dish into an interesting and memorable meal, and here are lots of ideas to choose from. Many of these sides are substantial and different enough to feature as snacks or light meals in their own right, and some, served in smaller portions, as appetisers. Choose from delicious vegetable and rice-based dishes, creative salads, and muffins and breads combining tasty savoury flavours.

4 Vegetables

There's no end to the wonderful things that can be done with the many fresh, seasonable vegetables now widely available. Use them in healthy and delicious curries and stir-fries, purées, bakes, tarts, frittatas and much more. Serve them in their own right or team them as an accompaniment to chicken, meat, seafood, eggs, rice or pasta dishes from other sections.

5 Chicken and seafood

Chicken stands alone for versatility! The number of delicious ways a whole bird, thighs, breasts, legs and wings can be used is extraordinary. Here are chicken recipes for any occasion you can imagine, with flavours enhanced by marinades, sauces, herbs and spices and the dishes often complemented by vegetables, rice and pasta. Fish and seafood, including prawns and scallops, also provides endless possibilities for great eating. The recipes in this section are simple but special: so good they're sure to become favourites.

6 Meat

If you love your meat, this section is a great resource, with a host of interesting ways to cook beef, lamb and pork. No more dinnertime dilemmas! These nutritious and flavoursome recipes include casseroles, roasts, stir-fries, grills, barbecues, curries and kebabs. Many of the recipes also feature vegetables, pasta or rice to turn the dishes into a full course.

7 Desserts and sweet treats

These goodies are not only ideal for rounding off a meal but can also serve as morning or afternoon tea, a snack, supper or a special treat. Choose from cakes, fritters, custards, puddings or tartlets and be tantalised by the imaginative range of sweet muffins and breads: delicious with butter or cream or on their own.

8 Index

Recipes are listed in several ways: alphabetically, by chief ingredients or principal flavours and by the type of dish. For example, 'Three bean rice salad' is listed under its name and under 'Salads', 'Beans' and 'Rice'.

Conversions

It's useful to know how to convert measurements and what oven temperatures equal, as these are often expressed differently from country to country. Conversions can be found on pages vii and viii, where this information is provided in a handy table format, and you'll also find tips on oven and microwave cooking times.

Conversions

Measurements differ from country to country, so it's important to understand what the differences are. This Measurements Guide gives you simple 'at-a-glance' information for using the recipes in this book, wherever you may be.

Cooking is not an exact science – minor variations in measurements won't make a difference to your cooking.

Equipment

There is a difference in the size of measuring cups used internationally, but the difference is minimal (only 2–3 teaspoons). We use the Australian standard metric measurements in our recipes:

1 teaspoon ... 5 ml
1 tablespoon ... 20 ml
½ cup ... 125 ml
1 cup ... 250 ml
4 cups ... 1 litre

Measuring cups come in sets of one cup (250 ml), ½ cup (125 ml), ⅓ cup (80 ml) and ¼ cup (60 ml). Use these for measuring liquids and certain dry ingredients.

Measuring spoons come in a set of four and should be used for measuring dry and liquid ingredients. When using cup or spoon measures always make them level (unless the recipe indicates otherwise).

Dry versus wet ingredients

While this system of measures is consistent for liquids, it's more difficult to quantify dry ingredients. For instance, one level cup equals: 200 g of brown sugar; 210 g of castor sugar; and 110 g of icing sugar.

When measuring dry ingredients such as flour, don't push the flour down or shake it into the cup. It is best just to spoon the flour in until it reaches the desired amount. When measuring liquids use a clear vessel indicating metric levels.

Always use medium eggs (55-60 g) when eggs are required in a recipe.

Dry		Liquids	
Metric (grams)	**Imperial (ounces)**	**Metric (millilitres)**	**Imperial (fluid ounces)**
30 g	1 oz	30 ml	1 fl oz
60 g	2 oz	60 ml	2 fl oz
90 g	3 oz	90 ml	3 fl oz
100 g	3½ oz	100 ml	3½ fl oz
125 g	4 oz	125 ml	4 fl oz
150 g	5 oz	150 ml	5 fl oz
185 g	6 oz	190 ml	6 fl oz
200 g	7 oz	250 ml	8 fl oz
250 g	8 oz	300 ml	10 fl oz
280 g	9 oz	500 ml	16 fl oz
315 g	10 oz	600 ml	20 fl oz (1 pint)*
330 g	11 oz	1000 ml (1 litre)	32 fl oz
370 g	12 oz		
400 g	13 oz		
440 g	14 oz		
470 g	15 oz		
500 g	16 oz (1 lb)		
750 g	24 oz (1½ lb)		*Note: an American pint is 16 fl oz.
1000 g (1 kg)	32 oz (2 lb)		

Oven

Your oven should always be at the right temperature before placing the food in it to be cooked. Note that if your oven doesn't have a fan you may need to cook food for a little longer.

Microwave

It is difficult to give an exact cooking time for microwave cooking. It is best to watch what you are cooking closely to monitor its progress.

Standing time

Many foods continue to cook when you take them out of the oven or microwave. If a recipe states that the food needs to 'stand' after cooking, be sure not to overcook the dish.

Can sizes

The can sizes available in your supermarket or grocery store may not be the same as specified in the recipe. Don't worry if there is a small variation in size – it's unlikely to make a difference to the end result.

Cooking temperatures	°C (celsius)	°F (fahrenheit)	Gas mark
very slow	120	250	1/2
slow	150	300	2
moderately slow	160	315	2–3
moderate	180	350	4
moderately hot	190	375	5
	200	400	6
hot	220	425	7
very hot	230	450	8
	240	475	9
	250	500	10

Nutritional value per serve Fat: 5.5 g Carbohydrate: 6.2 g Protein: 2.0 g

Parsnip and apple soup with garlic croutons

Preparation time 20 minutes Cooking time 30 minutes

Ingredients
2 tablespoons vegetable oil
1 onion, chopped
2 parsnips, chopped
1 cooking apple, chopped
2½ cups (600 ml, 1 pint) vegetable stock
2 tablespoons chopped fresh parsley
½ teaspoon dried marjoram
1¾ cups (440 ml, 14 fl oz) milk
salt and black pepper
extra parsley to garnish
Croutons
2 thick slices day-old white bread, crusts removed
1 large clove garlic, halved
2 tablespoons vegetable oil
serves 4

1 Heat oil in a large, heavy-based pan. Add onion and parsnips and cook for 5 minutes or until softened. Add apple, stock, parsley and marjoram and bring to the boil. Cover, reduce heat and simmer for 20 minutes or until the vegetables are tender.

2 Rub both sides of each slice of bread with a half-clove of garlic. Cut the bread into 1 cm (½-in.) cubes. Heat the oil in a heavy-based frying pan. Add the bread and fry for 2–3 minutes, until golden, stirring constantly. Drain on kitchen towels.

3 Remove soup from heat. Stir in the milk and season to taste. Blend until smooth in a food processor or with a hand blender. Reheat and serve with the croutons. Garnish with parsley.

Nutritional value per serve Fat: 1.9 g Carbohydrate: 7.7 g Protein: 5.2 g

Spicy lentil soup

Preparation time 10 minutes Cooking time 45 minutes

Ingredients
250 g (8 oz) dried split red lentils
1 litre ($1\frac{2}{3}$ pints) good quality vegetable stock
1 tablespoon vegetable oil
1 medium-sized onion, finely chopped
1 clove garlic, crushed
$2\frac{1}{2}$ cm (1-in.) knob of ginger, finely grated
2 teaspoons ground cumin
$\frac{1}{2}$ teaspoon cayenne pepper
salt and black pepper
juice of $\frac{1}{2}$ lemon
serves 4

1 Place lentils in a sieve and rinse under cold-running water, then place in a large pan. Pour over the stock. Bring to the boil, reduce heat, cover and simmer for 20 minutes.

2 Heat oil in a large frying pan, add onion and cook over a gentle heat, stirring occasionally, for 5 minutes or until softened. Add garlic, ginger, cumin and cayenne pepper and cook for a further minute.

3 Add the onion mixture to the lentils, season to taste. Cook for a further 20 minutes, or until lentils are soft. Add lemon juice, season to taste and serve.

Nutritional value per serve Fat: 6.4 g Carbohydrate: 11.3 g Protein: 5.6 g

Spinach and nutmeg soup with cheese toasts

Preparation time 25 minutes Cooking time 35 minutes

Ingredients
2 tablespoons olive oil
2 tablespoons butter
250 g (8 oz) floury potatoes, cut into chunks
250 g (8 oz) spinach leaves
1 teaspoon freshly grated nutmeg
salt and black pepper
1.4 litres (2½ pints) chicken or vegetable stock
4 tablespoons crème fraîche
100 g (3½ oz) gruyère cheese, grated
1 large egg, beaten
day-old narrow french bread stick, cut diagonally into 18 x 1 cm (½-in.) slices
serves 6

1 Heat oil and half the butter in a large pan. Fry potatoes for 1 minute, add spinach and nutmeg. Cook for 2 minutes, until spinach is wilting.

2 Add stock, season lightly and bring to the boil. Reduce heat, cover and simmer for 10–15 minutes, until potatoes are tender. Leave to cool for 10 minutes.

3 In a food processor, combine until smooth. Stir in half the crème fraîche, season to taste and set aside.

4 Preheat grill. Mix grated cheese, egg and remaining crème fraîche. Lightly toast the bread, spread cheese mixture on one side of each slice. Dot with remaining butter and season with black pepper. Grill for 5 minutes, until bubbling and golden. Return soup to pan and heat gently. Serve topped with cheese toasts.

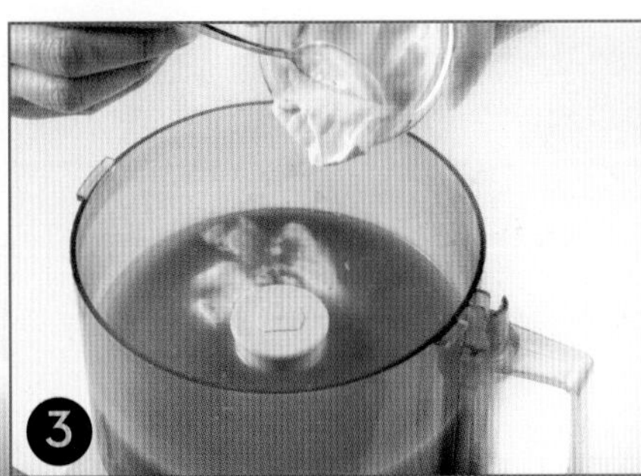

Nutritional value per serve Fat: 1.4 g Carbohydrate: 19 g Protein: 7.2 g

Japanese prawn and vegetable tempura

Preparation time 25 minutes, plus 20 minutes standing Cooking time 10 minutes

Ingredients
1 zucchini (courgette)
salt
4 green prawns
1 red capsicum (pepper)
1 large egg
150 g (5 oz) plain flour
1/2 cup (125 ml, 4 fl oz) ice-cold water
peanut oil for deep-frying
lime wedges to serve
soy sauce to serve

serves 4

1 Cut the zucchini in half across the centre, trim the end and cut each half lengthways into 4. Sprinkle with salt and set aside for 20 minutes. Shell the prawns, leaving tails attached. Devein, using a sharp knife. Rinse and refrigerate. Deseed the capsicum and cut into 8 strips.

1

2 Break the egg into a mixing bowl. Mix in the ice-cold water and fold in the flour to make a lumpy batter.

2

3 Heat 5 cm (2-in.) of oil in a wok or frying pan. Coat the zucchini slices in batter and deep-fry for 3 minutes or until golden, turning halfway through. Drain on kitchen towels and keep warm. Repeat with capsicum strips. Coat prawns and cook for 1 minute. Serve immediately with lime wedges and soy sauce.

3

Nutritional value per serve Fat: 4.3 g Carbohydrate: 38 g Protein: 8.5 g

Ricotta herb dip with garlic toasts

Preparation time 10 minutes Cooking time 10 minutes

Ingredients
6 pitted green olives, finely chopped
1 tablespoon chopped fresh tarragon
1 tablespoon chopped fresh chives
1 tablespoon chopped fresh mint
2 teaspoons finely grated lemon rind (zest)
250 g (8 oz) ricotta cheese
black pepper
4 tablespoons sun-dried tomato purée
1 large mixed grain baguette, cut into thick slices
1 clove garlic, halved
serves 4

1 In a large bowl combine olives, tarragon, chives, mint and lemon rind, and stir in ricotta. Season with pepper, mix well. Add tomato purée and stir gently to create a marbled effect. Spoon into a serving dish.

2 Preheat grill to high. Grill baguette slices for 1–2 minutes on each side, until golden. Rub garlic halves over toast slices and serve with ricotta dip.

1

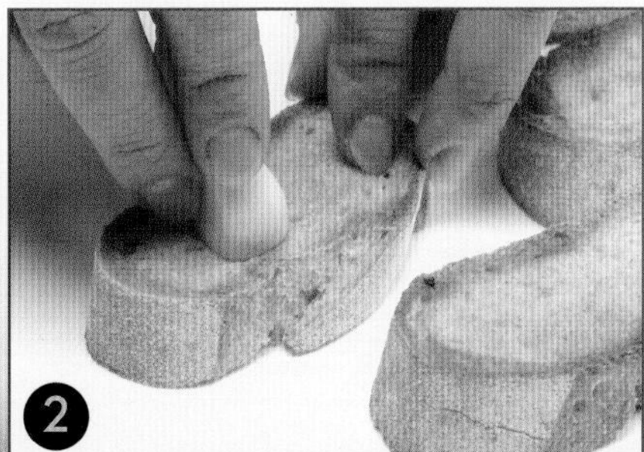

2

Nutritional value per serve Fat: 7.9 g Carbohydrate: 8.5 g Protein: 6.9 g

Potato cakes with smoked salmon

Preparation time 15 minutes Cooking time 40 minutes

Ingredients

- 300 g (10 oz) floury potatoes, unpeeled
- 150 ml (5 fl oz) milk
- salt and black pepper
- 1 large egg
- 30 g (1 oz) plain flour
- 4 spring onions, finely sliced
- 1 tablespoon oil
- 1/2 cup (125 ml, 4 fl oz) crème fraîche
- 2 tablespoons chopped fresh dill
- 150 g (5 oz) smoked salmon slices
- extra dill to garnish
- lemon wedges to serve

serves 4

1 Cook the potatoes in boiling salted water for 15–20 minutes, until tender, drain. Cool for a few minutes, then peel. Mash with milk, season, then beat in the egg, flour and spring onions to make a batter.

2 Heat a large non-stick frying pan, add a little of the oil. Make 4 potato cakes, using 2 tablespoons of batter for each. Fry for 2–3 minutes on each side until golden. Drain on kitchen towels and keep warm while you make 2 further batches of 4 potato cakes.

3 Combine the crème fraîche and chopped dill. Serve pancakes topped with the salmon slices and a spoonful of crème fraîche. Garnish with black pepper, dill and lemon.

Nutritional value per serve Fat: 25 g Carbohydrate: 13.6 g Protein: 12 g

Salami stacks

Preparation time 15 minutes, plus 2 hours refrigeration Cooking time 20 minutes

Ingredients

- 250 g (8 oz) cream cheese
- 90 g (3 oz) diced dried apricots
- 4 tablespoons mayonnaise
- ½ teaspoon tabasco sauce
- 16 slices danish salami
- extra 135 g (4½ oz) diced apricots, very finely chopped

makes 24

1 Bring cream cheese to room temperature, cream well, using a wooden spoon, to soften. Reserve 3 tablespoons cream cheese, leave at room temperature. Stir 90 g (3 oz) diced apricots, mayonnaise and tabasco into cream cheese.

2 Lay 4 salami slices on a clean board. Spread a heaped teaspoon of cheese mixture on each slice, making sure it is spread right to the edge. Place second salami slice on top and spread as above. Repeat with one more slice and top with the fourth slice. Place on a flat plate, cover with plastic wrap and refrigerate for 2 hours.

3 Spread the extra 135 g (4½ oz) of finely chopped apricots on kitchen paper in a 1½ cm-wide (½-in.) strip. Lightly spread reserved cream cheese around the sides of the salami stacks. Roll the sides of the stacks over the apricots, press on well. Cover and refrigerate. To serve, cut each stack into 6 triangles. Place a toothpick in centre of each and arrange on platter.

3

Nutritional value per serve Fat: 25.3 g Carbohydrate: 18.7 g Protein: 6.1 g

Apricot canapés

Preparation time 10 minutes

Ingredients

- 250 g (8 oz) cream cheese
- ½ cup (125 ml, 4 fl oz) mayonnaise
- 60 g (2 oz) chopped walnuts
- 2 teaspoons sherry (optional)
- 200 g (7 oz) large dried apricots

makes 25–30

1 In a large bowl, combine cream cheese and mayonnaise and mix until soft and fluffy. Add walnuts and sherry, and mix to combine.

2 Place a teaspoon of mixture onto each dried apricot and arrange on a platter. Serve at room temperature.

1

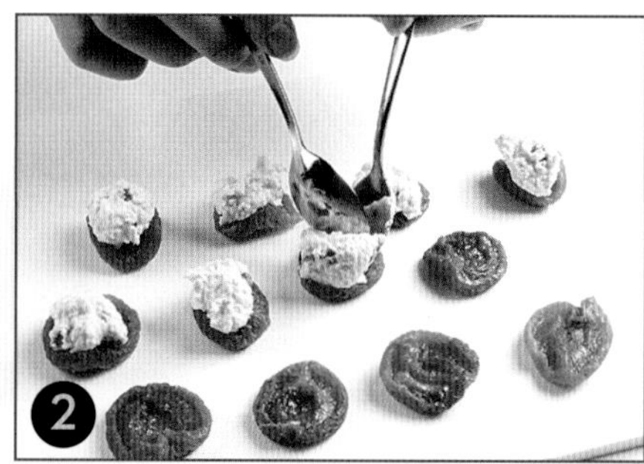

2

Nutritional value per serve Fat: 2.2 g Carbohydrate: 27.5 g Protein: 8.2 g

Prune and proscuitto rolls

Preparation time 5 minutes

Ingredients

150 g (5 oz) proscuitto

250 g (8 oz) pitted prunes

toothpicks

makes 24

1 Cut each proscuitto slice in half across the width and then in half again down its length.

2 Wrap a strip of proscuitto around each prune. Secure with a toothpick. Serve as an hors d'oeuvre.

Nutritional value per serve Fat: 9.2 g Carbohydrate: 15.8 g Protein: 6.2 g

Mini pizzas

Preparation time 35 minutes, plus 1–1½ hours standing time Cooking time 10 minutes

Ingredients

- 1 teaspoon active dry yeast
- pinch sugar
- ⅔ cup (170 ml, 5½ fl oz) warm water
- 250 g (8 oz) plain flour
- ½ teaspoon salt
- 4 tablespoons olive oil

Classic pizza topping

- 185 g (6 oz) tomato paste
- dried oregano leaves
- 315 g (10 oz) cherry tomatoes, sliced
- 125 g (4 oz) pepperoni or cabanossi, thinly sliced
- 20–25 pitted black olives, thinly sliced
- 250 g (8 oz) mozzarella cheese, grated

makes about 80

1 To make dough: In a small bowl, place yeast, sugar and water and mix to dissolve. Set aside in a warm place for 5 minutes or until mixture is foamy.

2 Place flour and salt in a food processor and pulse until combined. With machine running, slowly pour in yeast mixture and oil and process to make a rough dough. Turn dough onto a lightly floured surface and knead for 5 minutes or until soft and shiny. Add more flour if necessary.

3 Place dough in a lightly oiled bowl and roll around bowl to cover surface with oil. Cover bowl with plastic food wrap and place in a warm, draught-free place for 1–1½ hours or until doubled in size. Knock down and knead lightly.

4 Preheat oven to 190°C (375°F, gas mark 5). Divide dough into 4 cm (1½-in.) balls, press out to make 7 cm (2½-in.) circles and place on greased baking trays. Spread each dough circle with tomato paste, then sprinkle with oregano and top with slices of tomato, pepperoni or cabanossi and olives. Sprinkle with cheese and bake at 190°C (375°F, gas mark 5) for 10 minutes or until pizzas are crisp and brown.

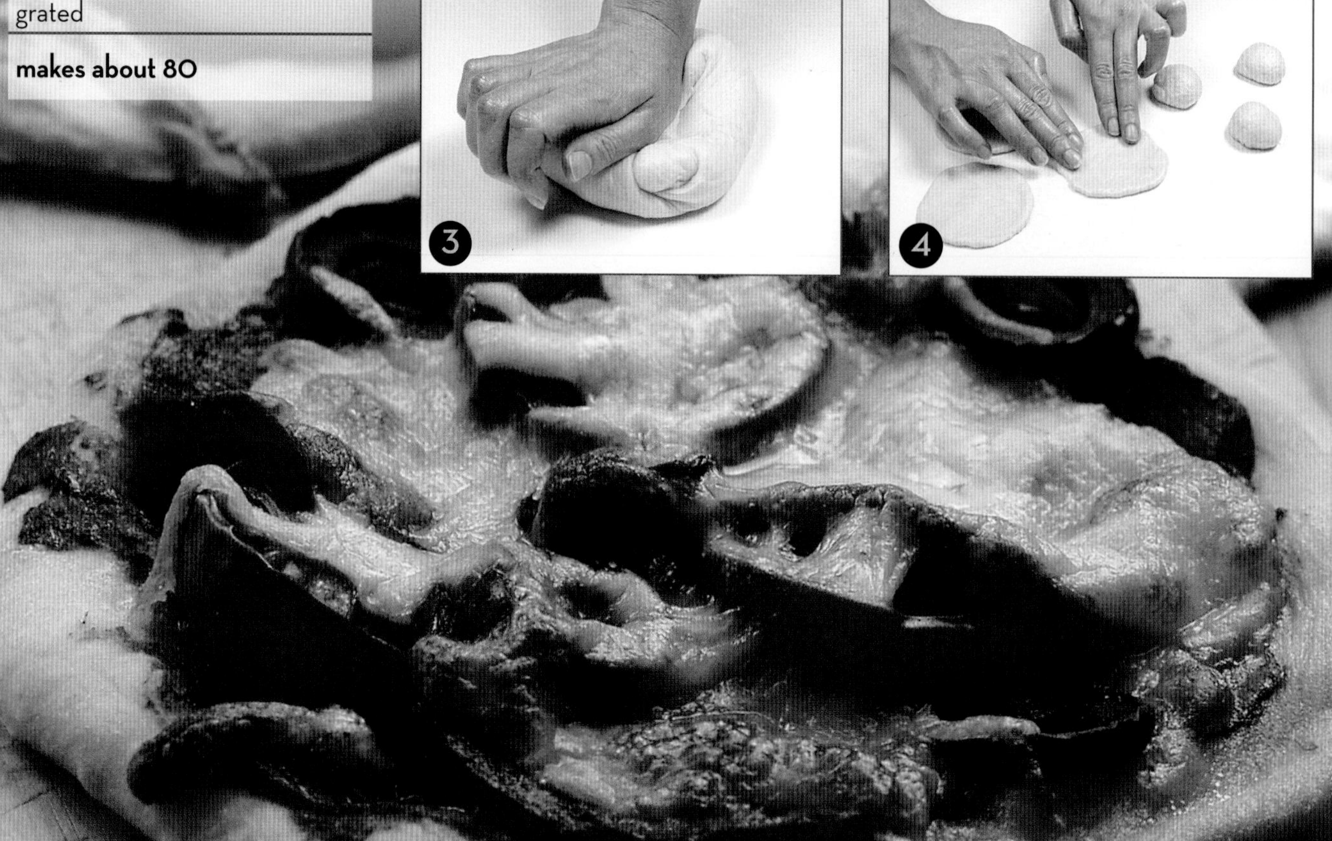

Nutritional value per serve Fat: 30.9 g Carbohydrate: 10.2 g Protein: 5.6 g

Samosas

Preparation time 15 minutes Cooking time 30–40 minutes

Ingredients
1 tablespoon vegetable oil
2 medium-sized onions, finely chopped
1 clove garlic, crushed
2 teaspoons curry paste
1/2 teaspoon salt
1 tablespoon white vinegar
250 g (8 oz) chicken mince
1/2 cup (125 ml, 4 fl oz) water
2 teaspoons sweet chilli sauce
2 tablespoons chopped coriander
1 packet large spring roll wrappers
1 1/2 cups (375 ml, 12 fl oz) vegetable oil

makes 30–36

1 Heat the wok to a medium-high heat. Add oil and fry onions and garlic until softened. Add curry paste and salt and stir to combine. Stir in vinegar. Add chicken mince for 3-4 minutes breaking up mince with the back of a spoon. Reduce heat, add water, cover and cook about 6 minutes until most of the water is absorbed. Add chilli sauce and coriander. Stir until the water has evaporated and mince is dry. Remove to a plate to cool. Rinse wok.

2 Cut 10 spring roll wrappers into 3 even strips. Place a teaspoon of filling at bottom end and fold over the pastry diagonally, forming a triangle. Fold again on the straight; continue to make 3 more folds in same manner. Moisten the inside edge of the last fold with water and press gently to seal.

3 Heat the clean wok. Add enough oil to be approximately 5 cm (2-in.) deep. Heat oil but take care not to overheat. Add 3 or 4 samosas and fry about 3-4 minutes until golden. Remove with a slotted spoon to a tray lined with paper towels. Repeat with remainder. If samosas become dark in colour, immediately remove from heat to drop the oil temperature.

1

2

Nutritional value per serve Fat: 7.5 g Carbohydrate: 11.4 g Protein: 13.3 g

Vietnamese spring rolls

Preparation time 10 minutes Cooking time 10–15 minutes

Ingredients
1 tablespoon oil
350 g (11½ oz) minced pork
1 tablespoon grated fresh ginger
1 tablespoon finely chopped spring onions
2 tablespoons soy sauce
1 small red chilli, deseeded and finely chopped
2 teaspoons honey
300 g (10 oz) green prawns, peeled, deveined and finely chopped
90 g (3 oz) bean sprouts
1 tablespoon chopped basil
24 wonton wrappers
oil for deep frying
makes 20

1 Heat oil in a frying pan over moderate heat. Add pork, ginger, spring onions and soy sauce. Cook while stirring constantly for 3 minutes. Stir in chopped chilli, honey, prawns, bean sprouts and basil, and mix well to combine. Remove to a flat dish, spread out to cool.

1

2 Separate wonton wrappers. Place on work surface and place a tablespoon of filling across the corner of each wrapper. Roll up, tucking in the sides. Brush end with water to seal.

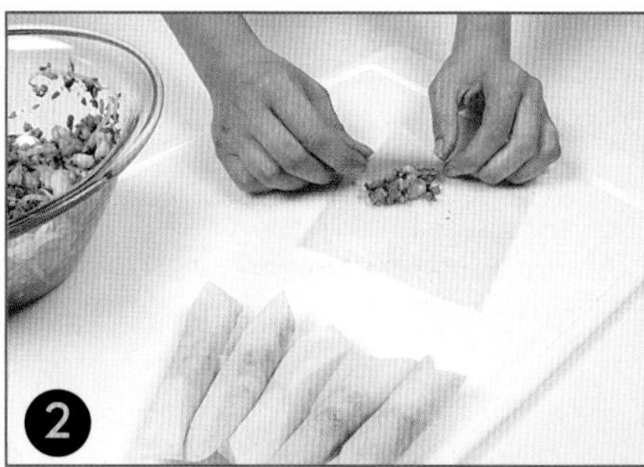
2

3 Heat enough oil to be 4 cm (1½-in.) deep in a saucepan. Add the rolls a few at a time and fry until golden. Drain on absorbent paper and continue with remainder. Serve hot.

3

Nutritional value per serve Fat: 13.1 g Carbohydrate: 14.1 g Protein: 11.9 g

Curried chicken rolls

Preparation time 20 minutes Cooking time 30 minutes

Ingredients

- 2 teaspoons canola oil
- 1 medium onion, finely chopped
- 1 small clove garlic, crushed
- 2 teaspoons mild curry paste
- 1½ tablespoons lemon juice
- 500 g (1 lb) chicken mince
- 3 tablespoons dried breadcrumbs
- ½ teaspoon salt
- ½ teaspoon pepper
- 2 tablespoons chopped fresh coriander
- 2 sheets frozen puff pastry, thawed
- 1 tablespoon milk for glazing
- 1 tablespoon sesame seeds

serves 16–20

1 Heat oil in a small pan, add onion and garlic and fry until onion is soft. Stir in curry paste and cook a little. Add lemon juice and stir to mix. In a bowl, combine the chicken, breadcrumbs, salt, pepper and coriander. Add the onion and curry mixture and combine well.

2 Preheat the oven to 190°C (375°F, gas mark 5). Cut each sheet of puff pastry in half across the centre. Pile a ¼ of the mince mixture in a thick 1½ cm (½-in.) wide strip along the centre of each pastry strip. Brush the exposed pastry at the back with water.

3 Lift the front strip of pastry over the filling and roll to rest onto the back strip. Press lightly to seal.

4 Cut the roll into 4 or 5 equal portions. Repeat the process with the remaining mince and pastry.

5 Glaze with milk and sprinkle with sesame seeds. Place onto a flat baking tray. Cook in the preheated oven for 10 minutes, reduce heat to 180°C (350°F, gas mark 4) and continue cooking for 15 minutes until golden brown. Serve hot as finger food.

Nutritional value per serve Fat: 5.7 g Carbohydrate: 12.4 g Protein: 15.0 g

Vindaloo chicken nuggets

Preparation time 20 minutes, plus 2 hours marinating Cooking time 15–18 minutes

Ingredients

- 1 kg (2 lb) chicken thigh fillets
- salt and pepper
- 1 tablespoon lemon juice
- 2 tablespoons vindaloo curry paste
- 125 g (4 oz) flour
- 2 eggs, lightly beaten
- 185 g (6 oz) dried breadcrumbs
- canola oil spray

Yoghurt and cucumber dipping sauce

- 1 lebanese cucumber, grated
- 1 cup (250 g, 8 oz) plain yoghurt
- 1 clove garlic, crushed
- 1 tablespoon lemon juice
- salt and pepper to taste

makes 32

1 Cut each thigh fillet into 4 pieces. In a bowl, place fillets and sprinkle lightly with salt and pepper. Pour over lemon juice. Toss to mix through. Rub the vindaloo curry paste well into each piece with your fingers. Cover and refrigerate 2 hours or more.

2 Preheat oven to 200°C (400°F, gas mark 6). Into shallow dishes or trays, place the flour, egg and breadcrumbs. Coat the chicken nuggets in flour, dip into the egg and press into the breadcrumbs to coat all sides. Lightly spray a large flat tray with canola oil spray. Place nuggets on the tray and spray the tops. Cook in a preheated oven for 15–18 minutes.

3 Into a strainer, place the cucumber and press to drain off excess liquid. Mix into the yoghurt. Add garlic, lemon juice, salt and pepper and place in a serving bowl. Serve with the hot nuggets.

Nutritional value per serve Fat: 10.3 g Carbohydrate: 22.4 g Protein: 8.7 g

Scallop puffs

Preparation time 10 minutes Cooking time 20 minutes

Ingredients

- 250 g (8 oz) scallops
- 4 tablespoons mayonnaise
- 60 g (2 oz) gruyère cheese, freshly grated
- ½ teaspoon dijon mustard
- 1 teaspoon fresh lemon juice
- 1 tablespoon finely chopped fresh parsley
- salt and pepper
- 1 large egg white
- 1 sheet puff pastry, cut into 25 squares (each 5 x 5 cm, 2 x 2-in.)

makes 25

1 Preheat oven to 160°C (315°F, gas mark 2–3). In a large pan combine scallops with salted water to cover completely, bring water to a simmer, and poach scallops for 5 minutes. Drain well and cut into 1 cm (½-in.) pieces.

2 In a large bowl, whisk together mayonnaise, gruyère, mustard, lemon juice, parsley, salt and pepper, add scallops, and toss mixture well. In a small bowl, beat the egg white until it forms stiff peaks. Fold into scallop mixture gently but thoroughly.

3 Prick squares and place on a lined oven tray. Bake for 5 minutes until lightly golden.

4 Preheat grill to medium-high. Remove pastry from oven and place a heaped teaspoon of the scallop mixture onto each. Place under grill and cook until golden and bubbling.

1

2

3

Nutritional value per serve Fat: 18.3 g Carbohydrate: 25.2 g Protein: 9.2 g

Chicken party sticks

Preparation time 15 minute Cooking time 25–30 minutes

Ingredients

- 500 g (2 lb) chicken tenderloins
- salt and pepper to taste
- 2 packets frozen puff pastry sheets
- 1 cup (250 ml, 8 fl oz) of bottled satay or sweet chilli sauce
- 2 tablespoons milk
- 1 tablespoon poppy or sesame seeds

makes 32

1 Preheat oven to 180°C (350°F, gas mark 4). Sprinkle salt and pepper over the chicken. Cut sheet of thawed pastry into 4 squares. Place a chicken tenderloin on each square and add a dash of your chosen sauce. Roll up on the diagonal, leaving ends open. Place seam-side down on a flat oven tray and glaze with milk. Sprinkle with poppy or sesame seeds.

2 Bake in preheated oven for 25–30 minutes. Serve hot as finger food with same sauce used as a dipping sauce.

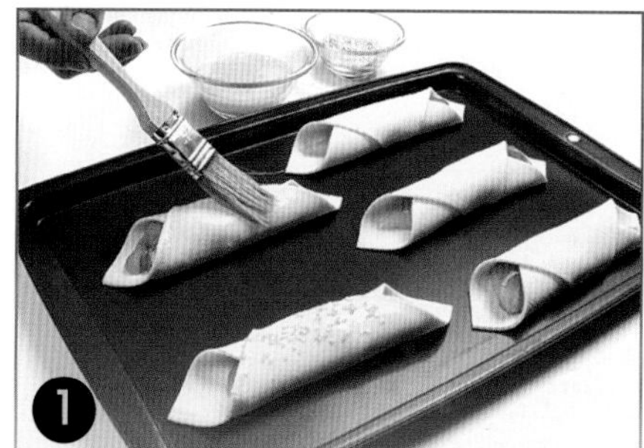

Nutritional value per serve Fat: 19 g Carbohydrate: 21 g Protein: 8.7 g

Mini savoury croissants

Preparation time 20 minutes Cooking time 12–15 minutes

Ingredients
250 g (8 oz) prepared puff pastry
1 egg
1 tablespoon water
butter for greasing
Asparagus and cheese filling
60 g (2 oz) gruyère cheese, grated
4 fresh asparagus spears, blanched and finely chopped
1/4 teaspoon ground paprika
black pepper

makes 12

1 Preheat oven to 200°C (400°F, gas mark 6). In a large bowl, combine cheese, asparagus, paprika and black pepper to taste.

2 Roll out pastry to 0.3 cm-thick (1/6-in.) and cut into 10 cm-wide (4-in.) strips. Cut each strip into triangles with 10 cm (4-in.) edge at the base.

3 Place a little filling across the base of each triangle, roll up from the base and mould into a croissant shape. In a small bowl, lightly beat egg with water then brush over croissant.

4 Place croissants on greased baking trays and bake for 12–15 minutes or until puffed and golden. Serve hot or cold.

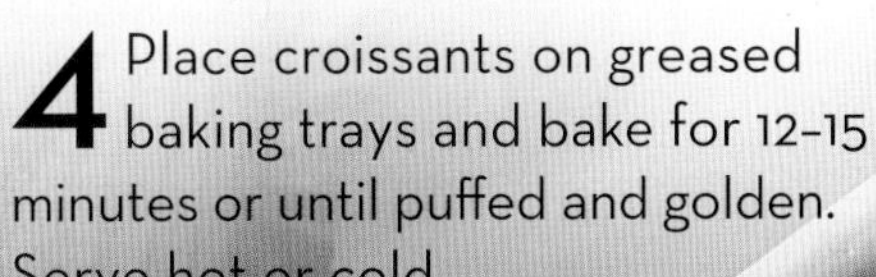

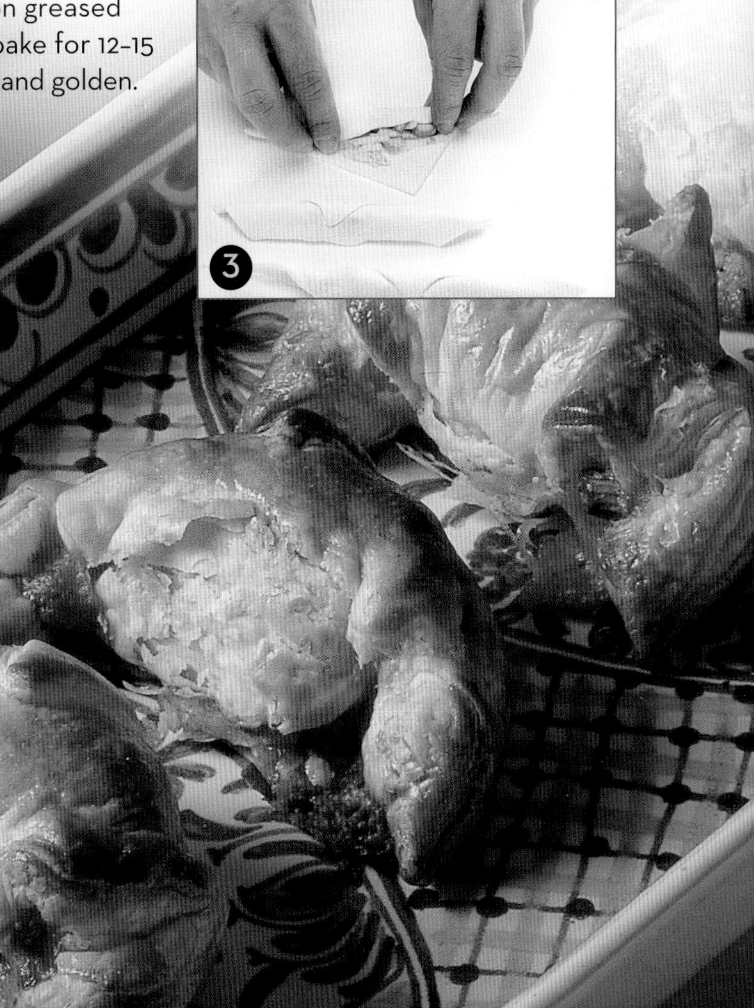

Nutritional value per serve Fat: 9.2 g Carbohydrate: 6.7 g Protein: 5.7 g

Roast pumpkin, potato and rosemary frittatas

Preparation time 15 minutes Cooking time 55 minutes

Ingredients

- 300 g (10 oz) butternut pumpkin, peeled, seeded and diced into 2 cm (3/4-in.) pieces
- 220 g (7 1/2 oz) potatoes, peeled and diced into 2 cm (3/4-in.) pieces
- 220 g (7 1/2 oz) sweet potatoes, peeled and diced into 2 cm (3/4-in.) pieces
- 1 tablespoon olive oil
- 2 sprigs rosemary, roughly chopped
- 1/2 teaspoon sea salt
- 4 eggs
- 1/2 cup (125 ml, 4 fl oz) thickened cream
- 1/2 cup (125 ml, 4 fl oz) milk
- 1 clove garlic, crushed
- 60 g (2 oz) parmesan cheese, grated
- salt and pepper to taste

serves 4

1 Preheat oven to 220°C (425°F, gas mark 7). Place pumpkin, potato, sweet potato, oil, half the rosemary and sea salt in a baking dish. Toss and bake for 20 minutes or until just cooked. Remove from oven and set aside.

2 Grease a 12 x 1 cup (250 ml, 8 fl oz) capacity muffin tin. Line bases with baking paper.

3 In a large bowl, combine eggs, cream, milk, garlic, parmesan, remaining rosemary and salt and pepper. Add potato, pumpkin and sweet potato. Reduce oven to 180°C (350°F, gas mark 4).

4 Pour mixture into muffin tins and bake for 30–35 minutes.

1

2

3

Nutritional value per serve Fat: 16.9 g Carbohydrate: 7.5 g Protein: 9.8 g

Thai fish cakes with peanut dipping sauce

Preparation time 20 minutes Cooking time 16 minutes

Ingredients

- 350 g (11½ oz) skinless cod fillets
- 1 tablespoon thai red curry paste
- 1 tablespoon thai fish sauce
- 2 tablespoons cornflour
- 1 medium egg, beaten
- 1 spring onion, finely chopped
- 60 g (2 oz) fine green beans, cut into 5 mm (¼-in.) lengths
- peanut oil for shallow-frying

Dipping sauce

- 2 tablespoons sugar
- juice of 1 lime
- 1 clove garlic, finely chopped
- 1 cm (½-in.) piece fresh root ginger, finely chopped
- 1 tablespoon roughly crushed roasted salted peanuts
- 1 small red chilli, deseeded and finely chopped
- 2 tablespoons light soy sauce

serves 4

1 In a food processor, finely mince the cod fillets. Add curry paste, fish sauce, cornflour and egg. Blend or stir until mixed. Transfer to a bowl and combine with spring onions and beans.

2 Lightly oil your hands (it's quite sticky), then divide mixture and shape into 8 patties. In a bowl, combine sugar and lime juice, stirring until sugar dissolves. Stir in garlic, ginger, peanuts, chilli and soy sauce. Set aside.

3 Heat 1 cm (½-in.) of oil in a large frying pan over a medium to high heat, then fry half of the fish cakes for 3–4 minutes on each side, until golden. Drain on kitchen paper, then cook remaining cakes. Serve with dipping sauce.

1

2

3

Nutritional value per serve Fat: 10.9 g Carbohydrate: 9.5 g Protein: 7.9 g

Spiced apricot meatballs

Preparation time 25 minutes, plus 1 hour soaking and 1½ hours refrigeration

Cooking time 30 minutes

Ingredients
140 g (4½ oz) diced dried apricots
2 tablespoons brandy
500 g (1 lb) beef mince
1 medium-sized onion, finely chopped
1 slice white bread, crusts removed and soaked in 4 tablespoons water
½ teaspoon ground cinnamon
pinch ground nutmeg
1 teaspoon salt
½ teaspoon pepper
1 egg
½ cup (125 ml, 4 fl oz) oil for frying
Apricot dipping sauce
90 g (3 oz) diced dried apricots
1 cup (250 ml, 8 fl oz) water
2 teaspoons sugar
2 teaspoons balsamic vinegar
1 teaspoon teriyaki sauce
1 teaspoon fresh ginger juice
makes 20–25

1 Soak the apricots in brandy for 1 hour. In a large bowl, place mince, onion, bread, cinnamon, nutmeg, salt, pepper and egg. Using hands, knead mixture until thoroughly combined. Cover and refrigerate for 1 hour.

2 Remove meatball mixture from refrigerator. Take a heaped teaspoon of mixture and roll into a ball with wet hands. Flatten slightly and press thumb in centre to form a deep depression. Place ¼ teaspoon soaked apricots in centre and remould into a ball, covering the apricot. Place on a flat tray and continue to roll the remainder. Cover with plastic wrap and refrigerate at least 30 minutes.

3 For the dipping sauce: Place diced apricots and water in a small pan with any remaining brandy-soaked apricots. Bring to the boil, reduce heat and simmer 15 minutes or until very soft. Stir in sugar, vinegar, teriyaki sauce and simmer 2 minutes. Purée in a blender or food processor. Stir in the fresh ginger juice and set aside.

4 Heat oil in a large, heavy-based frying pan. Fry meatballs in 2–3 batches, rolling them around the pan to cook all over and keep their shape (about 4–5 minutes each batch).

5 Drain on kitchen paper. Place on a heated serving platter, with dipping sauce in the centre and toothpicks for serving.

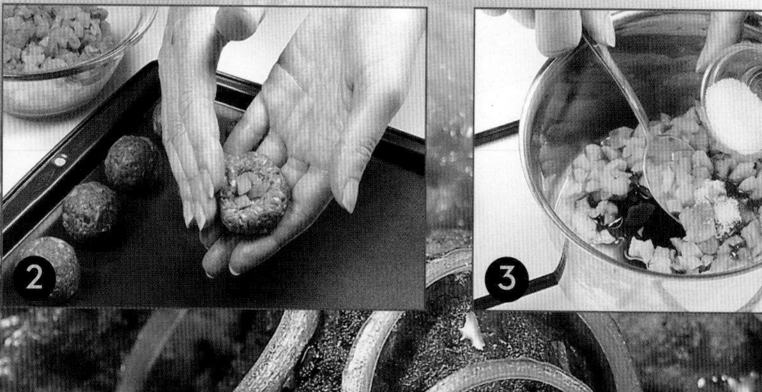

Nutritional value per serve Fat: 8.2 g Carbohydrate: 0.2 g Protein: 19.6 g

Moroccan lemon chicken shish kebabs

Preparation time 15 minutes, plus 30 minutes marinating Cooking time 10 minutes

Ingredients

500 g (1 lb) chicken breast fillets, trimmed of fat, cut into 2 cm (3/4-in.) cubes

Moroccan lemon marinade

- 1 tablespoon chopped parsley
- 1 tablespoon fresh rosemary leaves
- 2 teaspoons fresh thyme leaves
- 1 clove garlic, crushed
- 1 teaspoon black peppercorns, crushed
- grated rind (zest) and juice of 1 lemon
- 1 tablespoon olive oil
- 8 large metal or bamboo skewers

makes 8 kebabs

1 In a non-metallic bowl, place parsley, rosemary, thyme, garlic, black pepper, lemon juice and rind and oil. Add chicken. Toss to combine. Cover and refrigerate for at least 30 minutes.

2 Preheat barbecue or grill to a high heat. If using bamboo skewers, soak in cold water for at least 20 minutes.

3 Thread chicken onto skewers. Place on barbecue grill or under grill. Cook, brushing frequently with marinade and turning for 6–10 minutes or until chicken is cooked.

1

3

Nutritional value per serve Fat: 12.9 g Carbohydrate: 4 g Protein: 8.9 g

Balinese chicken satay

Preparation time 30 minutes, plus 2 hours marinating Cooking time 25 minutes

Ingredients

1 stalk lemongrass
1 onion, chopped
1 clove garlic, chopped
2 teaspoons ground coriander
1 teaspoon turmeric
juice of $^{1}/_{2}$ lemon
1 teaspoon salt
3 chicken breast fillets, cut into 1 cm ($^{1}/_{2}$-in.) cubes
$^{1}/_{2}$ cucumber, pared into ribbons with a vegetable peeler, to serve

Satay sauce

1 small onion, chopped
1 clove garlic, chopped
1 tablespoon peanut oil
1 teaspoon chilli powder
155 ml (5 fl oz) can coconut milk
75 g ($2^{1}/_{2}$ oz) roasted salted peanuts, finely ground
1 tablespoon soft dark brown sugar
1 tablespoon fresh lemon juice

serves 4

1 Peel the outer layer from the lemongrass and chop the bulbous part, discarding the fibrous top. Process to a paste with the onion, garlic, coriander, turmeric, lemon juice and 1 teaspoon of salt in a food processor.

2 Place the chicken in a non-metallic bowl and coat with the paste. Cover and marinate in the refrigerator for 2 hours, or overnight. If using wooden skewers, soak them in water for 10 minutes.

3 To make the satay sauce, process the onion and garlic to a paste in a food processor. Heat the oil in a heavy-based saucepan and fry the paste for 5 minutes, stirring. Mix in the chilli powder, then the remaining sauce ingredients. Bring to the boil, stirring, then simmer for 10 minutes.

4 Preheat the grill to high. Thread the chicken onto 8 skewers. Grill for 10 minutes, turning once, until cooked. Serve with cucumber ribbons and satay sauce.

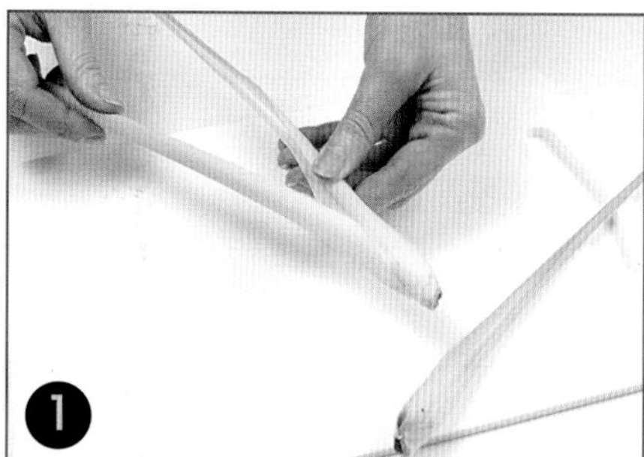
1

2

3

Nutritional value per serve Fat: 5.5 g Carbohydrate: 6.2 g Protein: 13.7 g

Lime-glazed chicken wings

Preparation time 10 minutes, plus 30 minutes marinating Cooking time 18 minutes

Ingredients

- 1 kg (2 lb) chicken wings, tips removed
- 4 tablespoons lime juice
- 1 tablespoon white-wine vinegar
- 2 tablespoons brown sugar
- 2 teaspoons soy sauce
- 2 tablespoons oil
- 4 spring onions, diagonally sliced
- 2 limes, thinly sliced
- ½ cup (125 ml, 4 fl oz) water
- 4 tablespoons white sugar
- ½ teaspoon white-wine vinegar

makes 12

1 Place chicken wings in a flat non-metal container. In a bowl, combine lime juice, vinegar, sugar and soy sauce. Pour over the wings and turn to coat. Marinate for 30 minutes or longer.

2 Heat the wok and add oil. Remove wings from marinade and stir-fry about 15 minutes until brown and tender. Add spring onions and stir-fry 1 minute. Pour in the marinade. Stir to coat and heat through. Remove to a platter and keep hot.

3 Add the lime and water to the wok and simmer 2 minutes. Stir in the sugar and vinegar, and cook until slices are coated with a thick syrup. Arrange slices over the wings. Pour over remaining syrup. Serve as finger food or as a meal with rice and vegetables.

Nutritional value per serve Fat: 17.9 g Carbohydrate: 6.3 g Protein: 13.2 g

Spicy deep-fried calamari rings

Preparation time 10 minutes, plus 2 hours marinating Cooking time 10 minutes

Ingredients

- 60 g (2 oz) plain flour
- 2 tablespoons paprika
- 1 teaspoon salt
- 500 g (1 lb) fresh calamari (squid), cut into rings
- vegetable oil for deep-frying

serves 4

1 In a large bowl, combine flour, paprika and salt. Toss the calamari rings in the seasoned flour to coat evenly. Set aside.

2 Heat 5 cm (2-in.) of vegetable oil in a large, heavy-based pan. Test that the oil is ready by adding a calamari ring – it should sizzle at once. Cook a quarter of the rings for 1–2 minutes, until golden. Drain on absorbent kitchen towels and keep warm while you cook the remaining rings in 3 more batches.

You'll never be short of ideas for satisfying family meals or something more sophisticated when you include those great staples of world cuisine: pasta, rice or noodles. This section suggests many exciting recipes for teaming them with meat, chicken, seafood or vegetables. You'll want to make these dishes again and again!

If you are looking to add complementary dishes to make a bigger course or meal, see the sections on Sides, Vegetables, Chicken and Seafood, and Meat.

Pasta

There are no hard and fast rules as to what kind of pasta to use for a particular dish. As a basic guide, however, hollow tube pastas such as penne or rigatoni are good for chunky, thick sauces while thin, flat pastas such as fettuccine and linguine are better suited to smooth, creamy sauces.

Cook pasta until it's 'al dente', i.e. until the pasta is soft but still slightly firm. (Note that fresh pasta cooks very quickly.) Drain it but do not rinse unless you're using it for pasta salad, and serve straight away. If you're making pasta salad, toss a little olive oil through to keep the strands separate.

As a rough guide, you'll need 60–80 g per person of fresh pasta and 90–100 g for dried pasta for starters. For mains, allow 100–125 g per person of fresh pasta and 125–150 g of dried pasta.

Rice

When calculating how much rice to cook, 1 cup of raw rice makes 3 cups of cooked rice. This quantity will serve 3–4 people. For six serves of cooked rice, 1½ cups of raw rice will be needed.

There are several varieties of rice commonly available, each best suited to particular foods or means of cooking.

Short and medium-grained rices have short, round kernels. When cooked, they are moist and sticky and tend to cling together. They are ideal for Chinese cooking, thickening soups, in stuffing, sushi, rice cakes, rice custard and creamed rice.

Long-grain rice has a long, thin kernel and remains well separated, dry and fluffy when cooked. Its somewhat plain flavour makes it ideal for rice salads and pilaffs, as it absorbs other flavours well.

Basmati rice has a long, narrow kernel and is prized for its fragrance and its nutty flavour. Although basmati is the preferred rice for Indian and Malaysian cooking, its flavour and firm-yet-tender texture when cooked make it suited to all cuisines. Jasmine rice is similar to basmati rice.

Arborio rice has a large, plump, rounded kernel. Arborio's distinctive, creamy texture makes it ideal for risottos, soups and rice puddings.

Brown rice has had its tough outer hull removed, leaving the bran layer covering the grain intact. Due to the bran, brown rice is more nutritious than white and takes longer to cook. Most varieties of rice can also be purchased in brown form.

Noodles

Dried rice noodles are also known as rice sticks or rice vermicelli. Bean thread noodles are also called cellophane noodles Cook these varieties by soaking them in hot water until soft and drain well, and then add them to stir-fries and soups.

Nutritional value per serve Fat: 3.9 g Carbohydrate: 20.7 g Protein: 2 g

Thick minestrone with pesto

Preparation time 15 minutes Cooking time 45 minutes

Ingredients
3 tablespoons olive oil
1 onion, chopped
2 cloves garlic, crushed
1 potato, cubed
2 small carrots, cubed
1 large zucchini (courgette), cubed
1/4 white cabbage, chopped
700 ml (1 1/4 pints) vegetable stock
2 x 400 g (13 oz) cans tomatoes, chopped
75 g (2 1/2 oz) pasta shells
salt and black pepper
4 tablespoons grated parmesan cheese
4 tablespoons pesto
serves 4

1 Place oil in a large pan, add onion, garlic, potato, carrots, zucchini and cabbage. Cook for 5–7 minutes, until softened.

2 Add stock and tomatoes and bring to the boil. Reduce heat and simmer for 20 minutes, add pasta shells and seasoning. Cook for a further 10 minutes, until pasta is al dente. Divide soup between bowls and top each serving with a tablespoon of parmesan and pesto.

1

2

Nutritional value per serve Fat: 7.7 g Carbohydrate: 21 g Protein: 8.8 g

Pasta primavera

Preparation time 15 minutes Cooking time 20 minutes

Ingredients

- 4 tablespoons butter
- 225 g (7½ oz) baby spinach
- 300 g (10 oz) fresh peas
- 300 g (10 oz) broad beans
- salt and black pepper
- 4 tablespoons crème fraîche
- 1 bunch spring onions, finely chopped
- 2 tablespoons finely chopped fresh parsley
- 90 g (3 oz) parmesan cheese, grated
- 400 g (13 oz) dried penne

serves 4

1 Melt butter in a pan, add spinach, cover, and cook for 2–3 minutes on medium high heat until wilted. Set aside to cool. Cook peas and beans in boiling water for 5 minutes, until tender. Drain and set aside.

2 Process spinach and crème fraîche in a food processor until smooth. Return purée to the pan, stir in peas and beans. Stir in spring onions and parsley. Season and add half the parmesan. Keep warm over a low heat.

3 Cook pasta in a large pan of boiling water. Drain, toss with spinach sauce. Sprinkle with the remaining parmesan.

Nutritional value per serve Fat: 7.3 g Carbohydrate: 8.7 g Protein: 6.7 g

Chicken and broccoli lasagne

Preparation time 20 minutes, plus 20 minutes standing time
Cooking time 40–45 minutes

Ingredients
900 ml (1½ pints) milk
2 shallots, sliced
2 sticks celery, sliced
2 bay leaves
250 g (8 oz) broccoli, cut into small florets
2 tablespoons sunflower oil
1 onion, chopped
1 clove garlic, crushed
250 g (8 oz) mushrooms, sliced
2 zucchini (courgettes), sliced
3 tablespoons butter
45 g (1½ oz) plain flour
125 g (4 oz) mature cheddar cheese, grated
320 g (11 oz) boneless chicken breasts, cooked and chopped
black pepper
180 g (6 oz) egg lasagne verdi sheets
serves 4–6

1 Place milk, shallots, celery and bay leaves in a pan, bring to the boil, remove from heat, stand for 20 minutes. Strain, discard shallots etc and reserve infused milk.

2 Cook broccoli in boiling water for 2 minutes. Drain and set aside.

3 Heat oil in a frying pan, sauté onion and garlic for 2-3 minutes until soft. Add mushrooms and zucchini, cook further 4-5 minutes. Set aside.

4 Preheat oven to 180°C (350°F, gas mark 4). Melt butter in a large pan, stir in flour to make a paste, add strained milk, bring to the boil, whisking. Reduce heat, simmer for 1-2 minutes until thickened. Set aside about a third of sauce. To the remaining sauce add half of the cheese, the broccoli and mushroom mixture, chopped chicken and black pepper.

5 Spoon half the mixture into a shallow ovenproof dish. Top with half the lasagne sheets. Repeat and pour over reserved sauce, sprinkle with remaining cheese. Bake for 40-45 minute, until golden and bubbling.

3

5

Nutritional value per serve Fat: 16.3 g Carbohydrate: 14 g Protein: 7 g

Meat ravioli with cream and parmesan

Preparation time 10 minutes Cooking time 15 minutes

Ingredients
600 g (1¼ lb) fresh beef ravioli
salt and black pepper
220 ml (7½ fl oz) thickened cream
2 tablespoons butter
freshly grated nutmeg
60 g (2 oz) parmesan cheese, grated
extra parmesan to serve
serves 4

1 Cook ravioli in a large pan of boiling water, until al dente. Place half the cream and the butter in a large frying pan. Heat gently for 1 minute or until butter has melted.

2 Drain ravioli, add immediately to cream and butter mixture. Cook for 30 seconds, stirring. Mix in remaining cream, nutmeg and parmesan. Season and toss for a few seconds, until well combined and heated through. Serve with extra parmesan.

Nutritional value per serve Fat: 9.5 g Carbohydrate: 40 g Protein: 15.2 g

Spaghetti carbonara

Preparation time 15 minutes Cooking time 20 minutes

Ingredients

185 g (6 oz) sliced ham, cut into strips

1/3 cup (90 ml, 3 fl oz) thickened cream

90 g (3 oz) parmesan cheese, grated

500 g (1 lb) dried spaghetti

freshly ground black pepper

serves 4

1 Heat a nonstick frying pan and cook ham on a medium heat for 2–3 minutes. Place eggs, cream and parmesan in a large bowl and beat lightly to combine. Set aside.

2 Cook spaghetti in a large pan of boiling water, until al dente. Place spaghetti in a large serving dish while still hot, add egg mixture and ham and toss, allowing the heat of the spaghetti to cook the sauce. Season with black pepper and serve.

Nutritional value per serve Fat: 13.1 g Carbohydrate: 26 g Protein: 7 g

Tagliatelle with asparagus and prosciutto

Preparation time 10 minutes Cooking time 20 minutes

Ingredients
500 g (1 lb) asparagus
4 tablespoons unsalted butter
2 tablespoons olive oil
1 spring onion, sliced
60 g (2 oz) proscuitto, cut into strips
150 ml (5 fl oz) thickened cream
salt and black pepper
500 g (1 lb) fresh tagliatelle
parmesan cheese, grated
serves 4

1 Cut asparagus spears into 3 cm (1-in.) pieces. Heat butter and oil in a large frying pan, add spring onion, cook for 2 minutes to soften, stir in proscuitto. Cook for 2 minutes, add asparagus and cook for 5 minutes, until softened. Pour in cream and bring to the boil, season to taste.

2 Cook pasta in a large pan of boiling water, until al dente. Drain and transfer to serving bowl, pour over the sauce. Sprinkle with parmesan.

Nutritional value per serve Fat: 4.1 g Carbohydrate: 25 g Protein: 13.2 g

Penne with chicken sauce

Preparation time 25 minutes Cooking time 20 minutes

Ingredients

- 2 teaspoons ground cumin
- 1 teaspoon olive oil
- 250 g (8 oz) mushrooms, sliced
- 470 ml (15 fl oz) jar pasta sauce
- 470 ml (15 fl oz) chicken stock
- 15 pitted black olives, finely chopped
- 400 g (13 oz) precooked chicken breast, cut into strips
- 250 g (8 oz) stir-fry vegetables (frozen or fresh)
- 400 g (13 oz) dried penne

serves 4–6

1 In a large frying pan heat oil, sauté cumin on a medium heat for 1 minute.

2 Add mushrooms, pasta sauce, chicken stock, olives, cooked chicken and vegetables. Cook for 5–6 minutes until vegetables are tender but crisp.

3 Cook pasta in a large pan of boiling water, until al dente. Drain well and set aside.

4 Serve pasta topped with chicken sauce.

Nutritional value per serve Fat: 3.8 g Carbohydrate: 18 g Protein: 6.8 g

Fruited chicken pasta salad

Preparation time 15 minutes Cooking time 20 minutes

Ingredients
250 g (8 oz) dried macaroni
250 g (8 oz) cooked chicken or turkey, chopped
320 g (11 oz) can tangerine or mandarin pieces
180 g (6 oz) seedless grapes, halved
1 stick celery, sliced
1/2 cup (125 ml, 4 fl oz) ranch-style salad dressing
pinch of pepper
1–2 tablespoons milk
4–5 iceberg lettuce leaves
250 g (8 oz) can water chestnuts, sliced
serves 4–6

1 Cook pasta in a large pan of boiling water, until al dente. Drain well and set aside.

2 In a large bowl combine cooked pasta, chicken or turkey, tangerines, grapes, water chestnuts and celery. Set aside.

3 In a small bowl combine ranch dressing and pepper. Pour over chicken mixture and toss lightly to coat.

4 Before serving, if necessary, stir in a little milk to moisten. Serve with lettuce cups.

Nutritional value per serve Fat: 7.5 g Carbohydrate: 21 g Protein: 5.2 g

Gingered thai rice salad

Preparation time 15 minutes Cooking time 15 minutes

Ingredients

- 2 cups (400 g, 13 oz) long-grain rice
- 1.5 litres (2½ pints) water
- 5 spring onions, finely sliced on the diagonal
- 3 medium carrots, coarsely grated
- 4 baby bok choy (pak choi), chopped
- 2 kaffir lime leaves, finely sliced
- 2 handfuls coriander, coarsely chopped
- 250 g (8 oz) roasted peanuts, chopped
- 1 tablespoon black sesame seeds
- 2 tablespoons chopped thai basil

Dressing

- 2 tablespoons vegetable or peanut oil
- 3 tablespoons lime juice
- 3 tablespoons thai fish sauce
- 2 tablespoons palm sugar
- 2 tablespoons sweet chilli sauce
- 1 tablespoon finely chopped ginger
- 1 pinch chilli powder or cayenne pepper
- salt and pepper to taste

serves 12

1 Cook rice in boiling salted water for 10–12 minutes or until tender. Drain and rinse thoroughly in cold water then drain again. In a bowl, whisk together dressing ingredients and set aside.

2 In a separate bowl, combine spring onions, carrots, bok choy, lime leaves, coriander, peanuts and sesame seeds.

3 Add the cooked rice and mix well. Toss thoroughly with the dressing, add thai basil and serve.

Nutritional value per serve Fat: 1.7 g Carbohydrate: 10 g Protein: 5.9 g

Seafood and broccoli risotto

Preparation time 15 minutes Cooking time 40 minutes

Ingredients

- 1 tablespoon sunflower oil
- 6 spring onions, chopped
- 1 clove garlic, finely chopped
- 1 red or yellow capsicum (pepper), diced
- 225 g (7½ oz) long-grain brown rice
- 2 cups (500 ml, 16 fl oz) vegetable stock
- 225 g (7½ oz) chestnut mushrooms, sliced
- 1 cup (250 ml, 8 fl oz) dry white wine
- 400 g (13 oz) marinara mix or frozen seafood mix, defrosted
- 225 g (7½ oz) broccoli, cut into small florets and boiled for 3 minutes
- 2 tablespoons chopped flat-leaf parsley
- salt and black pepper

serves 4

1 Heat the oil in a large saucepan. Add the spring onions, garlic and capsicum and cook for 5 minutes or until softened, stirring occasionally. Add the rice and cook for 1 minute, stirring, until well coated in the oil. In a separate pan, bring the stock to the boil.

2 Add the mushrooms, wine and ½ cup (125 ml, 4 fl oz) boiling stock to the rice mixture. Bring to the boil, stirring, then simmer, uncovered, for 15 minutes or until most of the liquid is absorbed, stirring often. Add another ¾ cup (185 ml, 6 fl oz) stock and cook for 15 minutes or until it is absorbed, stirring frequently.

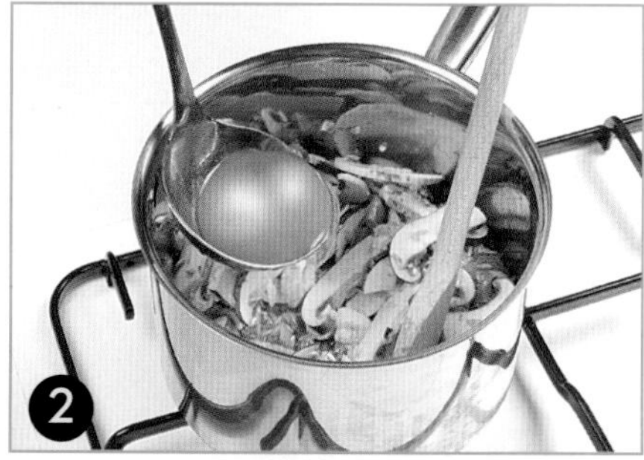

3 Add the seafood and most of the remaining stock. Stir frequently for 5 minutes or until the rice is cooked but firm to the bite. Add the rest of the stock, if necessary, and make sure the seafood is cooked through. Stir in the remaining broccoli, parsley, salt and pepper. Serve immediately.

Nutritional value per serve Fat: 6.5 g Carbohydrate: 20 g Protein: 11.7 g

Nasi goreng

Preparation time 10 minutes Cooking time 15–20 minutes, plus 1 hour cooling

Ingredients

250 g (8 oz) long-grain rice

1 litre (1 2/3 pints) boiling water

1 teaspoon ground turmeric

3 tablespoons vegetable oil

1 bunch spring onions, thinly sliced

2 1/2 cm (1-in.) fresh root ginger, finely chopped

1–2 red chillies, deseeded and thinly sliced

225 g (7 1/2 oz) pork fillet, thinly sliced

2 cloves garlic, crushed

3 tablespoons soy sauce, or to taste

200 g (7 oz) cooked peeled prawns, defrosted if frozen and thoroughly dried

juice of 1/2 lemon

coriander for garnish

serves 4

1 Cook the rice in boiling salted water, with turmeric added, for 12–15 minutes. Drain, then spread onto a large flat baking tray. Leave to cool for 1 hour or until completely cold, fluffing up occasionally with a fork.

2 Heat 2 tablespoons of the oil in a wok or heavy-based frying pan. Add half the spring onions, the ginger and chillies and stir-fry over a low heat for 2–3 minutes until softened. Add the remaining oil and increase the heat to high. Add the pork and garlic and stir-fry for 3 minutes.

3 Add the rice in 3 batches, stirring after each addition to mix well with the other ingredients. Add the soy sauce and prawns and stir-fry for 2–3 minutes until hot. Transfer to a bowl and mix in the lemon juice. Sprinkle with the remaining spring onions and garnish with coriander.

Nutritional value per serve Fat: 3.6 g Carbohydrate: 11.1 g Protein: 6.7 g

Fire and spice risotto

Preparation time 10 minutes Cooking time 30 minutes

Ingredients
800 g (1 lb 10 oz) skirt steak (beef flank)
4 tablespoons olive oil
8 cloves garlic, finely chopped or crushed
3 teaspoons fresh grated ginger
1 bunch of spring onions, chopped
2 small red chillies, finely chopped
2 teaspoons cumin
2 teaspoons ground coriander
2 teaspoons turmeric
400 g (13 oz) arborio rice
100 ml (3½ fl oz) red wine
100 ml (3½ fl oz) sherry
1 litre (1⅔ pints) beef stock, simmering
2 tomatoes, chopped
2 handfuls parsley, chopped
2 handfuls coriander, chopped
2 tablespoons lime juice
90 ml (3 fl oz) yoghurt
1 onion, finely sliced and deep-fried (optional)
extra chopped parsley
serves 4

1 Cut the skirt steak into 2.5 cm (1-in.) wide strips approximately 6 cm (2½-in.) long. Set aside.

2 Heat olive oil in a large, heavy-based saucepan. Add garlic, ginger, spring onions and chilli and stir over heat for 4 minutes. Add the beef strips and stir to brown on all sides. Stir in cumin, coriander and turmeric and stir 2 minutes. Add the rice and stir to coat the grains.

3 Add the wine, sherry and half of the hot stock. Bring to the boil while stirring, turn heat down to low, cover and simmer for 12 minutes. Stir in remaining hot stock, tomatoes, parsley and coriander. Cover and simmer for 8 minutes more. Turn off heat and stand covered 5 minutes.

4 Stir in the lime juice. Serve in individual bowls, garnished with a little yoghurt, a mound of fried onion and a sprinkling of parsley.

Nutritional value per serve Fat: 8.9 g Carbohydrate: 15.1 g Protein: 7.3 g

Persian-style pilaf

Preparation time 15 minutes Cooking time 25 minutes, plus 5 minutes standing

Ingredients

- 3 tablespoons olive oil
- 6 cloves garlic, crushed
- 2 large brown onions, roughly chopped
- 600 g (1¼ lb) lamb fillets, sliced
- 2 teaspoons cumin
- 400 g (13 oz) arborio rice
- 1 litre (1⅔ pints) vegetable stock, simmering
- 1 cinnamon stick
- 5 fresh dates, chopped
- 100 g (3½ oz) dried apricots, whole
- 10 prunes, whole
- 200 g (7 oz) walnuts, toasted and cut in half
- 2 tablespoons chopped coriander
- 2 tablespoons thick yoghurt
- 100 g (3½ oz) pistachio nuts, roughly chopped

serves 4–6

1 Heat the oil in a large saucepan. Add the garlic and onion and fry gently until onion is soft. Add the lamb and stir over high heat to brown, stir in the cumin.

2 Add the rice and quickly stir to coat the grains then stir in half of the hot stock. Add the cinnamon stick, turn heat down, cover and simmer 12 minutes or until liquid has just absorbed.

3 Add remaining hot stock, dates, apricots, prunes and walnuts. Cover and simmer 8 minutes or until rice is still a little firm. Turn off heat and stand covered for 5–8 minutes until liquid is absorbed. Remove the cinnamon stick, fluff the rice with a fork and stir in coriander.

4 Serve in individual warm bowls. Place a dollop of yoghurt on top and sprinkle with the pistachio nuts.

1

3

Nutritional value per serve Fat: 11.1 g Carbohydrate: 7.7 g Protein: 8.9 g

Cheesy baked rice

Preparation time 10 minutes Cooking time 40 minutes

Ingredients

- 2 tablespoons butter or margarine
- 2 leeks, sliced
- 3 rashers bacon, chopped
- ½ red capsicum (pepper), finely chopped
- 60 g (2 oz) long-grain rice, cooked
- 1 ½ cups (375 ml, 12 fl oz) milk
- 2 eggs, lightly beaten
- ½ teaspoon dry mustard
- 1 teaspoon worcestershire sauce
- 1 tablespoon mayonnaise
- 125 g (4 oz) mild cheddar cheese, grated
- 2 tablespoons chopped fresh parsley
- freshly ground black pepper
- 1 teaspoon paprika

serves 4

1 Preheat oven to 180°C (350°F, gas mark 4). Melt butter or margarine in a frying pan over a medium heat. Add leeks, bacon and capsicum and cook, stirring, for 4–5 minutes or until the leeks are soft and the bacon is brown. Mix with the rice and spoon mixture into a lightly greased ovenproof dish. Set dish aside.

2 Heat milk to hot but not boiling. In a bowl, whisk together the eggs, mustard, worcestershire sauce, mayonnaise, cheddar, parsley and black pepper.

3 Gradually whisk a few spoonfuls of hot milk into the egg mixture to temper the egg. Slowly pour in the remaining milk, while stirring.

4 Carefully pour the combined milk egg mixture into the dish containing the rice and leeks.

5 Place dish in a baking dish with enough hot water to come halfway up the sides. Bake in oven for 28–30 minutes or until custard is firm.

1

4

5

Nutritional value per serve Fat: 2.5 g Carbohydrate: 11.7 g Protein: 1.9 g

Chilli fried rice

Preparation time 20 minutes, including cooked rice Cooking time 8 minutes

Ingredients

- 2 teaspoons vegetable oil
- 2 fresh red chillies, chopped
- 1 tablespoon thai red curry paste
- 2 onions, sliced
- $1\frac{1}{2}$ cups (330 g, 11 oz) short-grain rice, cooked and cooled
- 125 g (4 oz) snake or green beans, chopped into $1\frac{1}{2}$ cm ($\frac{1}{2}$-in.) pieces
- 125 g (4 oz) baby bok choy (pak choi), blanched
- 3 tablespoons lime juice
- 2 teaspoons thai fish sauce

serves 4

1 Heat oil in a wok or frying pan over a high heat. Add chillies and curry paste and stir-fry for 1 minute or until fragrant. Add onions and stir-fry for 3 minutes or until soft.

2 Add rice, beans and bok choy to pan and stir-fry for 4 minutes or until rice is heated through. Stir in lime juice and fish sauce.

Nutritional value per serve Fat: 5.1 g Carbohydrate: 3.5 g Protein: 9.4 g

Beef with black bean sauce

Preparation time 15 minutes Cooking time 15 minutes

Ingredients

- 450 g (14 oz) sirloin or rump steak, cut into thin strips
- 1 clove garlic, crushed
- 1 small red chilli, deseeded and finely chopped (optional)
- 1 tablespoon dark soy sauce
- black pepper
- 2 teaspoons cornflour
- 1 tablespoon white-wine vinegar
- 2 tablespoons vegetable oil
- 1 red capsicum (pepper), deseeded and cut into strips
- 1 yellow capsicum (pepper), deseeded and cut into strips
- 1 large zucchini (courgette), cut into matchsticks
- 150 g (5 oz) snow peas (mangetout), sliced
- 3 tablespoons black bean stir-fry sauce
- 4 spring onions, diagonally sliced

serves 4

1 In a bowl, combine steak, garlic, chilli (if using), soy sauce and seasoning. In another bowl, mix cornflour with 1 tablespoon of water until smooth, stir in vinegar.

2 Heat the oil in a wok or large frying pan until very hot. Add the meat and its marinade and stir-fry for 4 minutes, tossing until seared on all sides.

3 Add capsicum and stir-fry for 2 minutes. Stir in zucchini and snow peas and cook for 3 minutes. Reduce the heat and add the cornflour mixture and black bean sauce. Stir to mix thoroughly and cook for 2 minutes or until the meat and vegetables are cooked through. Scatter with spring onions just before serving. Serve over egg noodles if desired.

1

2

3

Nutritional value per serve Fat: 3.8 g Carbohydrate: 6 g Protein: 3 g

Herbed rice noodles with asparagus and peanuts

Preparation time 20 minutes, plus 1 hour marinating Cooking time 4 minutes

Ingredients

- 3 tablespoons rice vinegar
- 1 tablespoon sugar
- 1 small spanish onion, finely sliced into rings
- 255 g (8 oz) dried rice noodles
- 2 bunches of asparagus
- a handful fresh mint, chopped
- a handful fresh coriander, chopped
- 1 continental cucumber, peeled, seeded and thinly sliced
- 6 spring onions, finely sliced
- 3 roma tomatoes, finely diced
- 120 g (4 oz) roasted peanuts, lightly crushed
- juice of 2 limes
- 2 teaspoons fish sauce
- 2 teaspoons olive oil
- $^1/_2$ teaspoon chilli flakes

serves 4

1 Whisk the rice vinegar and sugar together and pour over the onion rings. Allow to marinate for 1 hour, tossing frequently. Cook rice noodles in boiling water for 1–2 minutes then drain immediately and rinse under cold water. Cut into a manageable length with kitchen scissors.

2 Peel the tough skin off the lower third of the asparagus stalks with a potato peeler, then cut into 2 cm ($^3/_4$-in.) lengths. Simmer asparagus in salted water for 2 minutes until bright green and crisp-tender. Rinse in cold water to refresh.

3 Toss the noodles with the onion and vinegar mixture while still warm. Add asparagus, mint, coriander, cucumber, spring onions, tomatoes and roasted peanuts and toss thoroughly. In a small bowl, whisk the lime juice, fish sauce, oil and chilli flakes together and drizzle over the noodle salad. Serve at room temperature.

3

3

Nutritional value per serve Fat: 2.9 g Carbohydrate: 13.8 g Protein: 9.4 g

Stir-fry pork with bean sprouts and noodles

Preparation time 15 minutes Cooking time 10 minutes

Ingredients

- 450 g (14 oz) yellow or white fresh noodles
- 2–3 tablespoons fish sauce
- 1 cup (250 ml, 8 fl oz) chicken stock
- 1 teaspoon brown sugar
- 1/4 teaspoon white pepper
- 500 g (1 lb) pork stir-fry strips
- 2 tablespoons peanut oil
- 3 cloves garlic, crushed
- 1 onion, sliced
- 400 g (13 oz) mixed fresh bean sprouts, well washed
- 3 spring onions, cut into 1 cm (1/2-in.) lengths
- 12 sprigs fresh coriander
- 4 lime quarters

serves 4

1 Rinse the fresh noodles in hot water and drain well. In a bowl, combine fish sauce, chicken stock, sugar and pepper and set aside.

2 Heat wok and add 2 teaspoons oil. Stir-fry garlic until fragrant. Add half the pork and stir-fry to medium done. Remove, cook remainder adding more oil if needed and remove to a plate.

3 Add more oil, stir-fry onion for 1 minute. Add noodles, bean sprouts and stir-fry until hot. Add the pork and the stock mixture and toss. Add spring onions and coriander. Serve immediately with lime quarters.

Nutritional value per serve Fat: 7.3 g Carbohydrate: 13.3 g Protein: 3.5 g

Goan-style fish and coconut curry

Preparation time 15 minutes Cooking time 25 minutes

Ingredients
2 tomatoes
2 cardamom pods, husks discarded and seeds reserved
1 teaspoon ground coriander
1 teaspoon ground cumin
1 teaspoon ground cinnamon
1 teaspoon chilli powder
1/2 teaspoon ground turmeric
2 tablespoons vegetable oil
1 onion, finely chopped
1 clove garlic, finely chopped
2 1/2 cm (1-in.) piece fresh root ginger, finely chopped
400 ml (13 fl oz) coconut milk
fish fillet, such as haddock or cod, cut into 2 1/2 cm (1-in.) chunks
salt
steamed rice to serve
fresh coriander to garnish
serves 4

1 In a bowl, place the tomatoes and cover with boiling water. Leave to stand for 30 seconds. Skin and deseed the tomatoes, then dice. Crush the cardamom seeds using a mortar and pestle. To the mortar, add the coriander, cumin, cinnamon, chilli powder, turmeric and 2 tablespoons of water and mix to a paste. Set aside.

2 Heat a large wok. Add the oil and fry the onion, garlic and ginger for 3 minutes or until softened. Add the spice paste, mix well and fry for 1 minute, stirring.

3 Pour in the coconut milk and bring to the boil, stirring. Reduce the heat and simmer for 10 minutes or until the liquid has reduced slightly. Add the fish, tomatoes and salt to taste. Partly cover the wok and simmer for 10 minutes or until the fish turns opaque and is cooked through, stirring occasionally. Serve with steamed rice and garnish with coriander.

1

2

3

Nutritional value per serve Fat: 10.6 g Carbohydrate: 7.1 g Protein: 8 g

Pad thai with pork and prawns

Preparation time 20 minutes Cooking time 15 minutes

Ingredients

- 250 g (8 oz) rice noodles
- 4 tablespoons peanut oil
- 2 cloves garlic, chopped
- 1 shallot, chopped
- 125 g (4 oz) pork fillet, cut into 5 mm (1/4-in.) thick strips
- 1 tablespoon thai fish sauce
- 1 teaspoon sugar
- juice of 1/2 lime
- 1 tablespoon light soy sauce
- 1 tablespoon tomato sauce
- 200 g (7 oz) fresh bean sprouts
- 125 g (4 oz) cooked and peeled prawns
- black pepper
- 60 g (2 oz) roasted salted peanuts, chopped
- 1 tablespoon chopped fresh coriander
- 1 lime, quartered, to serve

serves 4

1 Prepare the rice noodles according to the packet instructions, rinse and drain well. Heat a wok. Add the oil, garlic, shallot and pork and stir-fry for 3 minutes or until the pork turns opaque. Stir in the rice noodles and mix thoroughly.

2 In a bowl, mix together the fish sauce, sugar, lime juice, soy sauce and tomato sauce. Add sauce mixture to the wok, stirring well. Stir-fry for 5 minutes. Mix in the bean sprouts and prawns and stir-fry for a further 5 minutes or until the bean sprouts are tender. Season with black pepper.

3 Transfer to a serving dish. Sprinkle over the peanuts and coriander, then serve with the lime wedges.

Sides are wonderful! They can be anything you want them to be and can play any role in your cooking plans. Light, interesting, highly adaptable dishes, these sides pair well with particular mains or act as support dishes to round out a meal. Some sides can solo as finger food, snacks and even starters.

The recipes in this section will suit all sorts of occasions. Discover sides that are vegetable-based – purées, wedges, fritters, salads and slices – and those containing dried beans, rice or pasta. Then there are savoury muffins and breads that you can enjoy on their own or that can complement soups and main salads.

You'll find more side dishes in the sections on Starters, Vegetables, Pasta, Rice and Noodles, and Desserts and Sweet Treats.

Salads at their best

For peak flavour, nutrition and appeal, salad greens and other salad vegetables should be served at their best. Here some tips for ensuring your salads are as fresh and crisp as possible:

- Only buy lettuces and leafy greens with crisp, shiny leaves. The base of the lettuce should be dry, not slimy.
- Store salad greens and vegetables correctly after you've purchased them. Do not wash them: place them immediately in the vegetable compartment of the refrigerator or on the lower shelves in a plastic bag or a covered plastic container or on a tray covered with a clean cloth or plastic wrap. It's important to cover their surface to prevent moisture loss.
- Greens that are bought tied in bunches – such as spinach, endive or rocket – should be opened and checked for dryness and wilting before being placed in the refrigerator.
- Before using salad greens, wash them thoroughly to remove all grit and drain them well. Dry the leaves before using, as dressing will not adhere to wet leaves and excess moisture will dilute the dressing. A salad spinner is excellent for getting rid of water or you can pat leaves dry with absorbent paper towel or shake them dry in a clean kitchen cloth.
- Crisper varieties of lettuce can be kept for up to 7 days, while softer leaf types will only last for 3–4 days. To crisp salad leaves, roll them up in a damp cloth and refrigerate them for an hour or until you are ready to serve.
- Ensure all vegetables and fruits are washed before cutting and cooking. Scrub root vegetables with a brush under running water to remove all dirt, particularly if they are to be eaten with the skin on.

Nutritional value per serve Fat: 9.7 g Carbohydrate: 32 g Protein: 20.9 g

Split lentil dhal with ginger and coriander

Preparation time 10 minutes Cooking time 40 minutes

Ingredients
200 g (7 oz) dried split red lentils
½ teaspoon turmeric
1 tablespoon vegetable oil
1 cm (½-in.) piece fresh root ginger, finely chopped
1 teaspoon cumin seeds
1 teaspoon ground coriander
salt and black pepper
4 tablespoons chopped fresh coriander
½ teaspoon paprika
extra coriander to garnish
serves 4

1 Rinse the lentils and drain well, then place in a large saucepan with 850 ml (1½ pints) of water. Bring to the boil, skimming off any scum, then stir in turmeric. Reduce the heat and partly cover the pan. Simmer for 30–35 minutes, until thickened, stirring occasionally.

2 Heat the oil in a small frying pan. Add ginger and cumin seeds and fry for 30 seconds or until cumin seeds start to pop. Stir in ground coriander and fry for 1 minute.

3 Season the lentils with salt and pepper, then add the toasted spices. Stir in the chopped coriander, mixing well. Transfer to a serving dish and garnish with the paprika and coriander leaves.

Nutritional value per serve Fat: 6.3 g Carbohydrate: 10.5 g Protein: 2.4 g

Zucchini polenta slices

Preparation time 15 minutes Cooking time 20 minutes, plus 1 hour cooling

Ingredients

- 1 tablespoon butter
- extra butter for greasing
- 3 tablespoons olive oil
- 250 g (8 oz) zucchini (courgettes), grated
- 3 cups, 750 ml (1¼ pints) chicken or vegetable stock
- 185 g (6 oz) instant polenta
- salt and black pepper
- 2 tablespoons grated parmesan cheese

serves 4

1 Grease a shallow 22 cm (8-in.) square roasting tin. Heat the butter and 1 tablespoon of oil in a large frying pan. Fry zucchini on a medium heat for 3–4 minutes, until softened but not browned, stirring frequently. Remove from heat and set aside.

2 Bring stock to the boil in a large pan. Sprinkle in polenta, stirring with a wooden spoon, and continue to stir for 5 minutes, until polenta thickens and begins to come away from the sides of the pan. Remove from the heat and stir in zucchini. Season to taste.

3 Turn polenta mix into the roasting tin, spreading evenly, sprinkle with parmesan and leave for 1 hour to cool and set.

4 Heat a ridged cast-iron grill pan over a high heat. Cut polenta into slices, brush with remaining oil and cook for 2–4 minutes on each side, until golden.

Nutritional value per serve Fat: 16.8 g Carbohydrate: 7.3 g Protein: 11.8 g

Roman kebabs

Preparation time 10 minutes, plus 10 minutes soaking Cooking time 10 minutes

Ingredients

- 1 french bread stick
- 400 g (13 oz) mozzarella cheese
- 4 tomatoes
- 1/3 cup (80 ml, 2 3/4 fl oz) olive oil
- 1 tablespoon lemon juice
- 1 teaspoon dried oregano
- salt and black pepper
- fresh basil to garnish

serves 4

1 Preheat oven to 230°C (450°F, gas mark 8). Soak 4 wooden skewers in water for 10 minutes.

2 Cut bread into thick slices, and cut mozzarella into 12 slices. Slice tomatoes into 3.

3 Combine oil, lemon juice, oregano and seasoning in a shallow dish. Brush both sides of bread with oil, thread bread onto skewers, alternating with mozzarella and tomato and finishing with bread. Pour over any remaining oil.

4 Place kebabs on a baking sheet, cook for 6–8 minutes, turning halfway through, until bread is crisp and cheese has melted. Serve garnished with basil.

Nutritional value per serve Fat: 6.6 g Carbohydrate: 11.3 g Protein: 4.1 g

Vine tomatoes and goat's cheese bruschetta

Preparation time 10 minutes Cooking time 15 minutes

Ingredients

- 450 g (14 oz) small vine-ripened tomatoes (with vine intact)
- 2 tablespoons extra virgin olive oil
- 1 clove garlic, crushed
- 4 sprigs fresh thyme
- 4 thick slices ciabatta, diagonally cut
- 4 tablespoons olive tapenade
- 100 g (3½ oz) soft goat's cheese, cut into chunks
- fresh basil to garnish

serves 4

1 Preheat oven to 220°C (425°F, gas mark 7). Place tomatoes in a large roasting tin and drizzle with oil. Sprinkle with garlic and thyme sprigs. Roast for 15 minutes, until tender. Divide tomatoes into 4 portions, each with vine intact, and set aside.

2 Preheat grill to high. Toast bread on both sides until golden. Spread each slice with 1 tablespoon of tapenade. Top with goat's cheese and tomatoes. Drizzle with juice from roasting tin and garnish with basil.

Nutritional value per serve Fat: 8.3 g Carbohydrate: 13.1 g Protein: 4.3 g

Grilled brie with beetroot salad

Preparation time 15 minutes Cooking time 10 minutes

Ingredients

- 1 avocado, sliced
- 250 g (8 oz) cooked beetroot, drained and chopped
- 2 celery sticks, sliced
- 1 red apple, cored and chopped
- 1 baguette, sliced into 4
- 125 g (4 oz) brie, quartered
- 120 g (4 oz) mixed salad leaves

Dressing

- 3 tablespoons extra virgin olive oil
- 3 tablespoons apple cider vinegar
- 1 clove garlic, crushed
- 1 red onion, finely chopped
- 1 tablespoon tomato purée
- sea salt and freshly ground black pepper
- 3 tablespoons pine nuts

serves 4

1 In a large bowl, place avocado, beetroot, celery and apple. Cover and set aside. Preheat grill to high and lightly toast bread for 2–3 minutes each side. Place a slice of brie on each piece, return to grill. Cook until cheese is melted and slightly golden.

2 Place all dressing ingredients in a small pan, bring to the boil and simmer for 2–3 minutes, until warmed through.

3 Divide salad leaves between four plates, top with beetroot mixture and a cheese toast. Drizzle with warm dressing and serve.

Nutritional value per serve Fat: 2 g Carbohydrate: 11.7 g Protein: 3.5 g

Sweet potato purée

Preparation time 10 minutes Cooking time 20 minutes

Ingredients

750 g (1½ lb) sweet potatoes, cut into large chunks

3 tablespoons milk

1 clove garlic, crushed

45 g (1½ oz) mature cheddar cheese, finely grated

1 tablespoon chopped fresh parsley

1 tablespoon snipped fresh chives

black pepper

extra chives to garnish

serves 4

1 Cook sweet potatoes in a large pan of boiling water for 10–15 minutes, until tender. Drain thoroughly, mash until smooth.

2 Heat milk in a small pan, add to potato along with garlic, cheddar, parsley, chives and black pepper. Beat until smooth and well combined. Serve garnished with fresh chives.

1

2

Nutritional value per serve Fat: 12.5 g Carbohydrate: 2 g Protein: 2.9 g

Asparagus and baby green beans with hazelnut dressing

Preparation time 15 minutes Cooking time 2 minutes

Ingredients

- 6 bunches asparagus, trimmed
- 1 kg (2 lb) baby green beans, topped and tailed
- 2 red capsicums (peppers), finely julienned

Dressing

- 4 tablespoons lemon juice
- 4 tablespoons white-wine vinegar
- 3 egg yolks
- 1 cup (250 ml, 8 fl oz) hazelnut oil
- 2 tablespoons chopped dill
- 160 g (5½ oz) toasted hazelnuts, chopped

serves 8–10

1 Bring a large pan of water to the boil. Add asparagus and beans and simmer for 1–2 minutes until just tender. Drain immediately and refresh in cold water, drain well.

2 Blend lemon juice, vinegar and egg yolks in a food processor until pale and creamy. Slowly drizzle in oil until the dressing comes together. Remove from processor and stir in dill and toasted nuts. Season to taste. Arrange all vegetables on a large platter in layers, drizzling each layer with dressing.

Nutritional value per serve Fat: 19.8 g Carbohydrate: 5.9 g Protein: 6.4 g

Potato feta fritters

Preparation time 10 minutes, plus 1–2 hours refrigeration Cooking time 10 minutes

Ingredients

- 245 g (7½ oz) potato, cooked and mashed
- 125 g (4 oz) feta cheese, crumbled
- 1 egg beaten
- 3 spring onions, chopped
- 3 tablespoons chopped fresh dill
- 1 tablespoon lemon juice
- finely grated rind (zest) of ½ lemon
- freshly ground black pepper
- flour, for dredging
- 4 tablespoons olive oil
- extra dill and lemon for garnish

serves 4

1 In a medium bowl, place the potato, feta, egg, spring onions, dill, lemon juice, rind and black pepper. Mix until well combined. Cover and refrigerate for 1–2 hours until firm.

2 Using hands, roll the mixture into golf-ball-size fritters, and flatten slightly. Dredge lightly in flour, using a small sieve.

3 Heat olive oil in a large frying pan. Cook fritters in batches for about 3–5 minutes until golden brown on both sides. Drain on a paper towel and serve immediately. Garnish with extra dill and lemon.

1

2

3

Nutritional value per serve Fat: 10.4 g Carbohydrate: 10.7 g Protein: 6.3 g

Pesto potato wedges

Preparation time 15 minutes Cooking time 40 minutes

Ingredients

4 medium-sized potatoes, peeled
2 tablespoons basil pesto
1 tablespoon olive oil
1 tablespoon water
60 g (2 oz) parmesan cheese, grated

serves 2–4

1 Preheat barbecue to high. Cut potatoes into wedges, rinse well and drain, then place in a large bowl. In a small bowl, combine basil pesto, olive oil and water. Pour over potatoes and toss to coat well. Place in a large foil dish in a single layer if possible.

2 Cook over indirect heat in a covered barbecue for 40 minutes, turning after 20 minutes.

3 Serve sprinkled with parmesan.

Nutritional value per serve Fat: 5.8 g Carbohydrate: 7.8 g Protein: 2.6 g

Roasted beetroot, orange and fennel salad

Preparation time 20 minutes Cooking time 1 hour

Ingredients

5 large beetroots
1 tablespoon brown sugar
1 teaspoon salt
2 tablespoons chopped fresh rosemary
3 tablespoons olive oil
1 bulb fennel
3 blood oranges, segmented
150 g (5 oz) hazelnuts, crushed and toasted

Dressing

1 handful dill, chopped
2 tablespoons balsamic vinegar
½ cup (125 ml, 4 fl oz) olive oil
salt and pepper

serves 4–6

1 Preheat the oven to 180°C (350°F, gas mark 4). Wash and trim the beetroots at root and stem ends leaving 1 cm (½-in.) of root and stem: do not peel. In a small bowl, combine sugar, salt, rosemary and 3 tablespoons olive oil until well blended. Add whole beetroots and toss in oil mixture. Wrap each beetroot in foil and place in a baking dish. Roast for approximately 1 hour until just tender.

2 Peel the beetroot by sliding off the skin with your fingers then cut into thick slices.

3 Trim tops and base of the fennel bulb and cut in half. Remove a wedge of tough core from each half making a 'v' cut at centre. Slice finely lengthwise. Mix with the segmented oranges pieces.

4 Combine the dill, balsamic vinegar, remaining olive oil and salt and pepper to taste. Whisk well until thick. Arrange beetroots on a serving platter with the thinly sliced fennel and orange. Drizzle over the dill vinaigrette, then scatter the hazelnuts on top.

Nutritional value per serve Fat: 2.4 g Carbohydrate: 3.3 g Protein: 2.3 g

Asian gingered coleslaw

Preparation time 20 minutes

Ingredients

Coleslaw

- ½ large savoy cabbage (curly cabbage), finely sliced
- 4 baby bok choy (pak choi), leaves separated and sliced
- 8 spring onions, julienned lengthways
- 200 g (7 oz) can sliced water chestnuts, drained
- 2 medium carrots, finely julienned
- 2 stalks lemongrass, finely sliced
- 4 kaffir lime leaves, finely sliced
- 1 bunch coriander, roughly chopped
- 90 g (3 oz) peanuts or sunflower seeds, crushed and toasted

Dressing

- 2 tablespoons mayonnaise
- 2 tablespoons yoghurt
- juice of 2 lemons
- juice of 1 lime
- 1 tablespoon grated fresh ginger
- 4 tablespoons rice vinegar
- salt and black pepper

serves 6

1 In a large bowl, combine cabbage, bok choy, spring onions, water chestnuts, carrots, lemongrass and lime leaves. Toss thoroughly.

2 In a jug, whisk together mayonnaise, yoghurt, lemon and lime juice, ginger, vinegar, salt and pepper until smooth. Pour over salad ingredients and toss thoroughly. Mix through coriander and sprinkle with peanuts or sunflower seeds.

1

2

Nutritional value per serve Fat: 4.7 g Carbohydrate: 7.4 g Protein: 1.3 g

Roasted vegetable salad

Preparation time 20 minutes Cooking time 35 minutes

Ingredients

- 3 red onions, quartered
- 3 potatoes, cut into wedges
- 2 zucchini (courgettes), thickly sliced
- 2 yellow capsicums (peppers), thickly sliced
- 4 tomatoes, halved
- 2 tablespoons olive oil
- sea salt and freshly ground black pepper
- shavings of parmesan cheese (optional)

Dressing

- 3 tablespoons extra virgin olive oil
- 2 tablespoons clear honey
- 1 tablespoon balsamic vinegar
- juice and finely grated rind (zest) of 1/2 lemon

serves 2–4

1 Preheat oven to 200°C (400°F, gas mark 6). Place all vegetables in a shallow roasting tin, drizzle with oil and season. Shake tray gently to coat vegetables. Bake for 35 minutes, until vegetables are tender and lightly browned.

2 In a small bowl combine all dressing ingredients. Pour over vegetables, tossing gently to coat. Serve topped with parmesan shavings.

1

2

Nutritional value per serve Fat: 10 g Carbohydrate: 9.6 g Protein: 2.4 g

Warm caramelised onion and herbed potato salad

Preparation time 10 minutes Cooking time 35 minutes

Ingredients

- $1\frac{1}{2}$ kg (3 lb) desiree or pontiac potatoes
- 2 tablespoons olive oil
- 4 white onions, sliced
- 1 handful fresh dill, chopped
- 1 handful fresh chervil, chopped
- 1 handful fresh parsley, chopped
- rind (zest) of 1 lemon
- salt and freshly ground black pepper

Dressing

- $\frac{2}{3}$ cup (170 ml, $5\frac{1}{2}$ fl oz) olive oil
- 3 tablespoons white-wine vinegar
- juice of 1 lemon
- 3 cloves garlic

serves 8–10

1 Scrub the potatoes to remove all traces of soil and cut into large chunks. Boil in water for 10 minutes until tender but not soft.

2 In a separate pan, heat 2 tablespoons oil and sauté onions over high heat for 2 minutes. Turn heat to low, cover and cook slowly for 20 minutes, stirring occasionally. Uncover, increase heat and stir until a rich caramel colour.

3 Drain potatoes and return to pan. In a jug, whisk white-wine vinegar, lemon juice, garlic and remaining oil until thickened. Pour over hot potatoes and toss. Add dill, parsley, chervil and lemon rind, and salt and freshly ground black pepper to taste. Add the caramelised onions and toss thoroughly. Serve immediately.

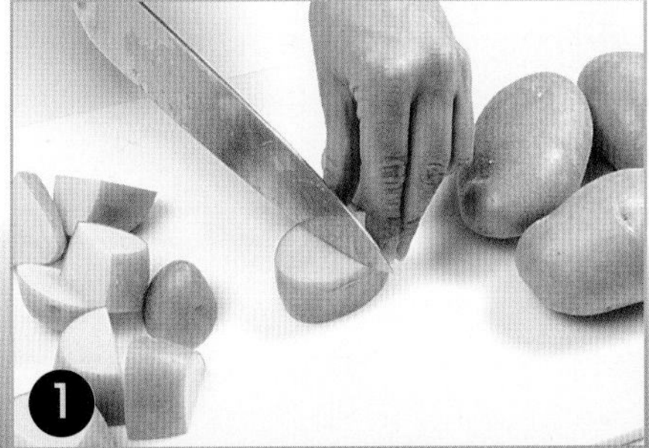

Nutritional value per serve Fat: 3 g Carbohydrate: 6.2 g Protein: 4.9 g

Warm butter bean and prosciutto salad with rocket

Preparation time 15 minutes Cooking time 5 minutes

Ingredients

- 420 g (14 oz) can butter beans
- 2 tablespoons olive oil
- 1/2 teaspoon dried chilli flakes
- 3 cloves garlic, finely chopped
- 100 g (3 1/2 oz) prosciutto, roughly chopped
- juice of 1 lemon
- 10 basil leaves, torn
- 1 bunch of rocket leaves
- salt and freshly ground black pepper

serves 6

1 Drain the canned beans in a strainer and rinse through with cold water.

2 Heat oil in a large frying pan. Add chilli flakes and garlic and sauté briefly until garlic is golden. Add prosciutto and for about 2 minutes stir over moderate heat until beginning to brown. Add butter beans and cook for 3 minutes, while tossing occasionally and adding lemon juice. Remove from heat.

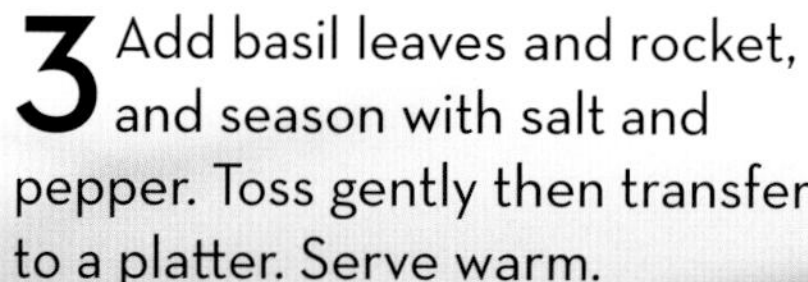

3 Add basil leaves and rocket, and season with salt and pepper. Toss gently then transfer to a platter. Serve warm.

Nutritional value per serve Fat: 13.9 g Carbohydrate: 6.8 g Protein: 3.6 g

Cabbage and chinese noodle salad

Preparation time 15 minutes Cooking time 5 minutes

Ingredients
Salad
1/2 savoy cabbage (curly cabbage), finely shredded
4 baby bok choy (pak choi)
8 spring onions, finely sliced
1/2 bunch coriander, roughly chopped
90 g (3 oz) flaked almonds, toasted
70 g (2 1/4 oz) pine nuts, toasted
100 g (3 1/2 oz) fresh chinese noodles
1 tablespoon peanut oil
Dressing
4 tablespoons peanut oil
2 tablespoons balsamic vinegar
2 tablespoons lime or lemon juice
1 tablespoon brown sugar
1 tablespoon soy sauce
salt and cracked pepper
serves 4–6

1 In a large bowl, place cabbage, spring onions and coriander. Slice bok choy widthways and add. Toss to combine.

2 Rinse, drain and then dry the chinese noodles in a clean towel. Heat 1 tablespoon of oil in a frying pan, add noodles and stir-fry for 2 minutes. Remove and allow to cool slightly.

3 In a salad bowl, combine the cabbage mixture, toasted nuts and fried noodles. Whisk vinegar, lime or lemon juice, sugar, soy sauce and remaining oil until thick. Add salt and pepper to taste. Pour over the dressing and toss well. Serve immediately.

Nutritional value per serve Fat: 1.5 g Carbohydrate: 21.1 g Protein: 5.5 g

Three bean rice salad

Preparation time 20 minutes Cooking time 18 minutes

Ingredients

- 250 g (8 oz) brown rice
- 185 g (6 oz) baby broad beans
- 400 g (13 oz) can black-eye (or other dried) beans, drained and rinsed
- 200 g (7 oz) can red kidney beans, drained and rinsed
- 1 red capsicum (pepper), chopped
- 1 bunch spring onions, chopped
- fresh coriander to garnish

Dressing

- 155 ml (5 fl oz) tomato juice
- 1 tablespoon olive oil
- 1 tablespoon white-wine vinegar
- 2 teaspoons dijon mustard
- 1 clove garlic, crushed
- 2 tablespoons chopped fresh coriander
- black pepper

serves 4

1 Bring a large pan of water to the boil. Add rice and cook for 12 minutes, stirring occasionally. Drain. Cook broad beans in a pan of boiling water for 4–5 minutes until tender. Rinse under cold water and drain, removing skins if desired. Rinse rice under cold water, drain and place in large serving bowl.

2 Place tomato juice, olive oil, vinegar, mustard, garlic, coriander and black pepper in a small bowl and whisk until combined.

3 Pour dressing over the rice and toss to combine. Add broad beans, black-eye beans, kidney beans, capsicum and spring onions and toss well. Cover and refrigerate before serving. Garnish with fresh coriander.

Nutritional value per serve Fat: 5.4 g Carbohydrate: 16 g Protein: 4.2 g

Risotto with baby spinach and gorgonzola

Preparation time 10 minutes Cooking time 25 minutes

Ingredients
1 litre (1 2/3 pints) chicken stock
2 tablespoons olive oil
2 cloves garlic, crushed
1 onion, finely chopped
2 cups (440 g, 14 oz) arborio rice
125 ml (4 fl oz) white wine
225 g (7 1/2 oz) baby spinach
225 g (7 1/2 oz) gorgonzola cheese, in small pieces
salt and freshly ground pepper

serves 6

1 In a saucepan, place stock and bring to the boil. Leave simmering. Heat oil in a large saucepan. Add garlic and onion, and cook for 5 minutes until soft. Add rice and stir until well coated. Pour in wine and cook until the liquid has been absorbed.

2 Add the stock to the saucepan, a ladle at a time, stirring continuously until liquid has been absorbed before adding the next ladle of stock. Keep adding stock this way, and stirring, until all the stock is used and the rice is cooked, but still a little firm to bite.

3 Add the spinach, gorgonzola, salt and pepper. Stir until spinach is wilted and cheese has melted. Serve immediately.

Nutritional value per serve Fat: 0.1 g Carbohydrate: 26 g Protein: 0.1 g

Fragrant pilaf

Preparation time 5 minutes Cooking time 20 minutes

Ingredients

- large pinch of saffron strands
- 1 tablespoon boiling water
- 2 tablespoons butter
- 1 golden shallot, finely chopped
- 3 cardamom pods
- 1 cinnamon stick
- 1¼ cups (250 g, 8 oz) basmati rice, rinsed and drained
- 400 ml (13 fl oz) hot water
- pinch salt

serves 4

1 Soak the saffron strands with 1 tablespoon water and set aside. Melt the butter in a large, heavy-based saucepan. Fry the shallot gently for 2 minutes or until softened. Add the cardamom pods, cinnamon and rice and mix well.

2 Add the hot water, salt and strain in the saffron liquid. Bring to the boil, then reduce the heat and cover the pan tightly. Simmer for 15 minutes or until the liquid has been absorbed and the rice is tender. Remove the cardamom pods and cinnamon stick before serving. Serve to accompany grilled fish or chicken.

1

2

Nutritional value per serve Fat: 14.3 g Carbohydrate: 26 g Protein: 5.6 g

Penne with capsicum and marscarpone

Preparation time 10 minutes Cooking time 15 minutes

Ingredients

- 2 tablespoons olive oil
- 1 clove garlic, crushed
- 2 red onions, chopped
- 1 green capsicum (pepper), chopped
- 1 red capsicum (pepper), chopped
- 1 yellow capsicum (pepper), chopped
- 400 g (13 oz) dried penne
- 200 g (7 oz) mascarpone
- juice of 1/2 lemon
- 4 tablespoons chopped flat-leaf parsley
- black pepper
- 4 tablespoons grated parmesan cheese (optional)

serves 4

1 Heat oil in large frying pan. Cook garlic, onions and capsicums for 5–10 minutes on medium-low heat, stirring frequently, until vegetables have softened. Cook pasta in a large pan of boiling water, until al dente. Drain and set aside.

2 Add half the mascarpone, the lemon juice, parsley and seasoning to the capsicum mixture. Stir to combine. Cook on medium heat until mascarpone melts.

3 Add remaining mascarpone to pasta, mix to combine. Pour mixture into pasta, toss well. Serve sprinkled with parmesan.

Nutritional value per serve Fat: 9.4 g Carbohydrate: 12.2 g Protein: 4.3 g

Sweet potato and peanut salad

Preparation time 15 minutes Cooking time 40 minutes

Ingredients

2 kg (4 lb) sweet potato, peeled
6 tablespoons olive oil
20 cloves garlic, unpeeled
salt and pepper
1 spanish onion, finely chopped
1–2 small red chillies, finely chopped
2 handfuls fresh herbs of your choice
2 tablespoons balsamic vinegar
320 g (11 oz) roasted peanuts
salt and freshly ground pepper

serves 10–12

1 Peel and cut the sweet potato into large chunks. Toss with 2 tablespoons of olive oil and place in a large baking dish with the garlic cloves. Season to taste with salt and pepper. Bake at 220°C (425°F, gas mark 7) for about 40 minutes or until sweet potato is tender and golden around the edges. Remove from the oven.

1

2 Place cooked sweet potato on a platter, mix the spanish onion, chilli, fresh herbs together and sprinkle over the sweet potato.

2

3 Whisk the remaining olive oil with the salt and pepper and balsamic vinegar, drizzle over the sweet potato. Sprinkle the peanuts over and gently toss the salad. Serve immediately.

3

Nutritional value per serve Fat: 11.2 g Carbohydrate: 24 g Protein: 5.5 g

Potato sour cream muffins

Preparation time 15 minutes Cooking time 30 minutes

Ingredients

- 250 g (8 oz) mashed potato
- 2 eggs, lightly beaten
- 1 cup (250 ml, 8 fl oz) milk
- 3/4 cup (185 ml, 6 fl oz) sour cream
- 4 tablespoons butter, melted
- 315 g (10 oz) self-raising flour, sifted
- 3 tablespoons snipped fresh chives

makes 6

1 Preheat oven to 180°C (350°F, gas mark 4). In a large bowl, combine potatoes, eggs, milk, sour cream and butter.

2 In a separate bowl, combine flour and chives. Add to potato mixture and mix until just combined.

3 Spoon mixture into 6 greased 1-cup (250 ml, 8 fl oz) capacity muffin tins and bake for 25–30 minutes or until muffins are cooked when tested with a skewer. Turn onto wire racks to cool.

3

Nutritional value per serve Fat: 7.9 g Carbohydrate: 35 g Protein: 6.7 g

Fresh herb and oat scones

Preparation time 20 minutes Cooking time 20 minutes

Ingredients

- 185 g (6 oz) self-raising flour, sifted
- 45 g (1½ oz) instant oats
- ½ teaspoon baking powder
- 2 tablespoons butter
- 2 teaspoons chopped fresh parsley
- 2 teaspoons chopped fresh basil
- 2 teaspoons chopped fresh rosemary
- ¾ cup (190 ml, 6 fl oz) skim milk

makes 9

1 Preheat oven to 220°C (425°F, gas mark 7). In a large bowl, place flour, oats and baking powder. Rub in butter using fingertips until mixture resembles fine breadcrumbs. Stir in parsley, basil and rosemary.

2 Make a well in the centre of the mixture and pour in milk. Mix lightly with a knife until all ingredients are just combined. Turn mixture out onto a lightly floured board and knead lightly.

3 Gently roll dough out evenly to 2 cm (¾-in.) thickness. Cut into rounds using a 5 cm (2-in.) floured pastry cutter. Arrange side by side in a lightly greased 18 cm (7-in.) round shallow baking tin. Brush tops with a little extra milk and bake for 15–20 minutes or until risen and golden. Turn onto a wire rack to cool.

Nutritional value per serve Fat: 22.4 g Carbohydrate: 22 g Protein: 12.6 g

Blue cheese and walnut damper

Preparation time 20 minutes Cooking time 40 minutes

Ingredients

310 g (10 oz) self-raising flour, sifted

220 g (7½ oz) blue cheese, crumbled

1 tablespoon snipped fresh chives

1 teaspoon paprika

155 g (5 oz) walnuts, chopped

1 cup (250 ml, 8 fl oz) buttermilk or milk

1 tablespoon walnut or vegetable oil

60 g (2 oz) parmesan cheese, grated

makes 1

1 Preheat oven to 180°C (350°F, gas mark 4). In a large bowl, combine flour, blue cheese, chives, paprika and 125 g (4 oz) walnuts.

2 Make a well in the centre of flour mixture, add milk and oil and mix to form a soft dough.

3 Turn dough onto a lightly floured surface and knead until smooth. Roll into a large ball, flatten slightly and place on a lightly greased baking tray. Sprinkle with parmesan and remaining walnuts. Bake for 40 minutes or until golden and risen.

1

2

3

Nutritional value per serve Fat: 12.4 g Carbohydrate: 31 g Protein: 9.7 g

Sun-dried tomato and provolone quick bread

Preparation time 25 minutes Cooking time 50 minutes

Ingredients
4 tablespoons olive oil
2 tablespoons sugar
2 large eggs
2 cloves garlic, crushed
$1^{1}/_{4}$ cups (360 ml, 10 fl oz) buttermilk
375 g (12 oz) unbleached bread flour
2 teaspoon baking powder
$^{1}/_{2}$ teaspoon bicarbonate of soda
$1^{1}/_{2}$ teaspoons salt
125 g (4 oz) provolone or other sharp yellow cheese, grated
60 g (2 oz) spring onions, thinly sliced
30 g (1 oz) fresh parsley, chopped
1 teaspoon freshly ground black pepper
80 g (3 oz) sun-dried tomatoes, chopped
serves 4–6

1 In a large bowl, combine the oil, sugar, eggs, garlic and buttermilk until smooth.

2 In a separate bowl, combine the flour, baking powder, bicarbonate of soda and salt, then add cheese, spring onions, parsley, pepper and tomatoes.

3 Add the buttermilk mixture to the flour mixture and stir until just combined.

4 Pour the batter into a greased 20 cm x 10 cm (8 x 4-in.) loaf tin, smooth top with a wet spoon and bake for 50 minutes or until risen and golden. Cool for 10 minutes then remove from tin.

The amazing thing about vegetables is they are so delicious, light and versatile, but also so nutritious! Rich in vitamins, minerals and dietary fibre, vegetables are the cornerstone of a healthy diet, so we need to eat several varieties every day.

Vegetables offered by supermarkets, greengrocers and specialty outlets are endless in their variety, taste, texture and colour. There's no danger of running out of ideas for including vegetables for everyday meals or special occasions.

Try recipes that pair appropriate vegetables with pulses, pasta, soups, eggs, cheese and pastry and consult the sections on Sides and Pasta, Rice and Noodles for further ideas on super ways with vegetables. If you are looking for ideas for vegetables served with main meals, see the sections on Chicken and Seafood, and Meat.

Buying and storing

Freshness is an important factor in relation to vegetables. For maximum taste and goodness, try to buy only what you need. It's better to purchase a few of these staples regularly rather than as part of a big, once-weekly shop. Plan meals with in-season vegetables so that they are at their best. Frozen vegetables have their place too, especially if you can't shop regularly. Add frozen varieties to soups and simmering dishes.

When buying fresh vegetables, be fussy and choose carefully. Purchase only those with no signs of spoilage. Avoid potatoes, onions, carrots, pumpkin, beetroot, sweet potato, parsnips, turnips and swedes with blemished skin or marks, a musty smell or that have started to soften or sprout. Brassicas – broccoli, cabbage, cauliflower and Brussels sprouts – are quick to show signs of being past their best, so look for those that are still at their peak.

Crisp vegetables should be just that. Try bending beans, snow peas or sugar snap peas prior to purchase. Fennel, asparagus and celery should be crisp with upright stalks. Capsicum should be shiny and heavy for their size and mushrooms should have a fresh, earthy aroma and tight caps. Check mushrooms sold in trays covered with plastic for signs of decay.

Store salad greens in plastic bags or wrapped in wetted paper towels in the crisper section of your refrigerator. If there is not enough room, put them on the lower shelves in a plastic bag or on a covered plastic container or tray. The important thing is to cover their surface to prevent moisture loss.

Root vegetables should be stored on a rack in a well-ventilated dark place. Apart from some root vegetables, vegetables generally and salad greens should be consumed as soon as possible, within a few days. The section on Sides also covers the storage of salad greens and vegetables.

Nutritional value per serve Fat: 0.3 g Carbohydrate: 2.7 g Protein: 1.4 g

Roasted capsicum and tomato soup

Preparation time 15 minutes, plus 10 minutes cooling Cooking time 35 minutes

Ingredients

- 3 red capsicums (peppers), halved and deseeded
- 1 onion, unpeeled and halved
- 4 large plum tomatoes
- 4 cloves garlic, unpeeled
- 1⅓ cups (350 ml, 11 fl oz) chicken or vegetable stock
- 1 tablespoon tomato purée
- salt and black pepper
- 2 tablespoons chopped fresh parsley

serves 4

1 Preheat oven to 200°C (400°F, gas mark 6). Place the capsicums and onion on a baking sheet, cut-side down, add whole tomatoes and garlic. Cook in the oven for 30 minutes or until tender and well browned.

2 Remove from oven and cool for 10 minutes, then peel, discarding skins. Place the vegetables in a food processor with half the stock and process until smooth.

3 Return to the pan, add the remaining stock and tomato purée, stirring to combine, then bring to the boil and cook until heated through. Season to taste and garnish with parsley just before serving.

1

2

Nutritional value per serve Fat: 7.2 g Carbohydrate: 2.9 g Protein: 2.3 g

Provençal-style soup with spring onion pesto

Preparation time 20 minutes Cooking time 25 minutes

Ingredients
2 tablespoons extra virgin olive oil
1 onion, chopped
1 medium potato, peeled and chopped
1 carrot, chopped
1 yellow capsicum (pepper), deseeded and chopped
2 cups (500 ml, 16 fl oz) vegetable stock
2 celery sticks, chopped
2 zucchini (courgettes), chopped
400 g (13 oz) can tomatoes, chopped
1 tablespoon tomato purée
sea salt
freshly ground black pepper
Pesto
6 spring onions, chopped with green part
60 g (2 oz) parmesan cheese, grated
4 tablespoons extra virgin olive oil
serves 4–6

1 For the soup: heat oil in a large, heavy-based pan, add onion, potato, carrot and capsicum. Cook uncovered for 5 minutes over a medium heat, stirring occasionally, until vegetables begin to brown.

2 Add the stock, celery and zucchini and bring to the boil. Cover, reduce heat and simmer for 10 minutes or until the vegetables are tender. Stir in tomatoes, tomato purée and season generously. Simmer uncovered for 10 minutes.

3 For the pesto: place spring onions, parmesan and oil in a food processor and process to a fairly smooth paste. Ladle soup into bowls and top with a spoonful of pesto.

2

3

Nutritional value per serve Fat: 1.7 g Carbohydrate: 3.4 g Protein: 1.4 g

Indian-spiced potato and onion soup

Preparation time 10 minutes Cooking time 40 minutes

Ingredients
1 tablespoon vegetable oil
1 onion, finely chopped
1 cm (1/2-in.) piece fresh root ginger, finely chopped
2 large potatoes, cut into 1 cm (1/2-in.) cubes
2 teaspoons ground cumin
2 teaspoons ground coriander
1/2 teaspoon turmeric
1 teaspoon ground cinnamon
1 litre (1 2/3 pints) chicken stock
salt and black pepper
1 tablespoon natural yoghurt to garnish
serves 4

1 Heat the oil in a large saucepan. Fry onion and ginger on a medium heat for 5 minutes or until softened. Add potatoes and fry for a further minute, stirring often.

2 In a small bowl combine the cumin, coriander, turmeric and cinnamon with 2 tablespoons of cold water to make a paste. Add to the onion and potato, stirring well, and fry for about 1 minute.

3 Add the chicken stock and season to taste. Bring to the boil, reduce heat, cover and simmer for 30 minutes or until the potato is tender. Blend until smooth in a food processor or press through a metal sieve. Return to the pan and gently heat through. Garnish with the yoghurt and extra black pepper.

1

2

3

Nutritional value per serve Fat: 7.1 g Carbohydrate: 5.5 g Protein: 1.4 g

Tomatoes yemistes

Preparation time 25 minutes Cooking time 1 hour, 10 minutes

Ingredients
12 medium-sized ripe tomatoes, washed
2 teaspoons sugar
salt and pepper
extra 1/2 teaspoon sugar
1/2 cup (125 ml, 4 fl oz) olive oil
1 large onion, finely chopped
45 g (1 1/2 oz) pine nuts
1 1/4 cups (280 g, 8 oz) short-grain rice
75 g (2 1/2 oz) currants
1 1/2 cups (375 ml, 12 fl oz) hot water
2 tablespoons chopped flat-leaf parsley
2 tablespoons chopped mint
makes 12

1 Slice the top of each tomato almost through. Flip back the lid and scoop out the pulp with a teaspoon. Sprinkle each cavity with a pinch of sugar, place in a baking dish and set aside. Into a saucepan, place tomato pulp with salt, pepper and 1/2 teaspoon sugar. Simmer until pulp is soft. Press through a sieve, discard seeds. Set purée aside.

2 In a saucepan, heat 4 tablespoons oil and fry the onion until soft. Add pine nuts and stir 2 minutes. Add rice, stir a little to coat grains. Add currants, hot water, parsley, mint and 1/2 cup (125 ml, 4 fl oz) tomato purée. Bring to the boil, turn down heat, cover and simmer gently 10–12 minutes, until all liquid is absorbed.

3 Preheat oven to 180°C (350° F, gas mark 4). Spoon rice mixture into tomatoes, allowing a little room for rice to swell. Replace lid. Pour remaining tomato purée over the tomatoes and add about 1/2 cup (125 ml, 4 fl oz) water to the dish.

4 Spoon remaining oil over the tomatoes and place, uncovered, into oven for 40–60 minutes or until rice is tender. Check liquid, if drying out, add a little extra water. Serve tomatoes with their sauce.

Nutritional value per serve Fat: 8.8 g Carbohydrate: 6.1 g Protein: 1.9 g

Spring vegetables in spiced coconut curry

Preparation time 20 minutes Cooking time 35 minutes

Ingredients

- 1 stalk lemongrass, peeled and white part finely chopped
- 2 tablespoons vegetable oil
- 1 cm (1/2-in.) piece fresh root ginger, chopped
- 1 onion, finely chopped
- 1 clove garlic, finely chopped
- 1 teaspoon turmeric
- 225 g (7 1/2 oz) potatoes, cut into 2 cm (3/4-in.) chunks
- 2 carrots, thickly sliced
- 400 ml (13 fl oz) can coconut milk
- 2 bay leaves
- 1 red chilli, deseeded and finely chopped
- salt
- 125 g (4 oz) baby sweetcorn, cobs, fresh or frozen
- 170 g (5 1/2 oz) fine green beans
- 2 zucchini (courgettes), thickly sliced
- 2 tablespoons chopped fresh coriander

serves 4

1 Heat the oil in a large, heavy-based saucepan. Add lemongrass, ginger, onion and garlic and fry for 5 minutes or until the onion and garlic have softened. Stir in turmeric, potatoes and carrots, then add the coconut milk, bay leaves, chilli and salt. Bring to the boil, reduce the heat and simmer, partly covered, for 10 minutes, stirring occasionally.

2 Add sweetcorn and beans and simmer, partly covered, for 10 minutes. Add the zucchini and cook for a further 10 minutes or until all the vegetables are tender. Remove the bay leaves and garnish with coriander just before serving.

Nutritional value per serve Fat: 7.8 g Carbohydrate: 2.9 g Protein: 3.3 g

Green vegetable stir-fry with sesame seeds

Preparation time 10 minutes Cooking time 15 minutes

Ingredients
2 tablespoons sesame seeds
2 tablespoons peanut oil
1 clove garlic, roughly chopped
2½ cm (1-in.) piece fresh root ginger, finely chopped
150 g (5 oz) broccoli, cut into very small florets, peel and slice the thick stems
2 zucchini (courgettes), halved lengthways and finely sliced
170 g (5½ oz) snow peas (mangetout)
1 tablespoon rice wine or medium-dry sherry
1 tablespoon dark soy sauce
1 tablespoon oyster sauce
serves 4

1 Heat a wok, add sesame seeds and dry-fry for 2 minutes until golden, shaking the wok frequently. Remove and set aside. Add oil to the hot wok, then add garlic and ginger and stir-fry over a medium heat for 1–2 minutes until softened. Add broccoli and stir-fry for a further 2–3 minutes.

2 Add the zucchini and snow peas and stir-fry for 3 minutes. Pour over the rice wine or sherry and sizzle for a minute. Add the soy and oyster sauces, mix well and stir-fry for 2 minutes. Sprinkle over toasted sesame seeds just before serving.

1

2

Nutritional value per serve Fat: 6.9 g Carbohydrate: 1.6 g Protein: 5.2 g

Tofu and bok choy

Preparation time 10 minutes, plus 2 hours marinating Cooking time 10 minutes

Ingredients

315 g (10 oz) firm tofu, cut into 2 cm (3/4-in.) cubes
60 g (2 oz) walnuts, roughly chopped
1 tablespoon finely grated fresh ginger
1 tablespoon chopped fresh coriander
4 tablespoons japanese soy sauce
1 teaspoon sesame oil
2 tablespoons vegetable oil
1 bunch (about 500 g, 1 lb) bok choy (pak choi), chopped
1 bunch (500 g, 1 lb) chinese broccoli, chopped
1 tablespoon oyster sauce
1 tablespoon sweet chilli sauce

serves 4

1 In a bowl, combine tofu, walnuts, ginger, coriander, soy sauce and sesame oil. Cover and marinate at room temperature for 2 hours. Drain, reserving marinade.

2 Heat 1 tablespoon vegetable oil in a wok over a medium heat. Add bok choy and broccoli and stir-fry for 3 minutes or until just tender. Remove to a serving platter and keep warm.

3 Heat remaining oil in wok, add tofu and walnuts and stir-fry for 5 minutes or until tofu is golden. Add reserved marinade and oyster and chilli sauces, then stir-fry for 2 minutes. Place on top of vegetables. Serve immediately.

Nutritional value per serve Fat: 6 g Carbohydrate: 2.2 g Protein: 2.9 g

Warm spinach salad with walnuts

Preparation time 5 minutes Cooking time 2 minutes

Ingredients

- 1 tablespoon walnut oil
- 1 red onion, sliced into thin rings
- 5 sun-dried tomatoes in oil, drained and chopped
- 500 g (1 lb) baby spinach
- 3 tablespoons walnut pieces
- salt
- 3 tablespoons chopped fresh coriander to garnish

serves 4

1 Heat the oil in a wok, add the walnuts and stir-fry for 30 seconds. Add the onions and cook for a further 30 seconds.

2 Add the tomatoes, spinach and salt to taste. Cook for 1 minute or until the spinach begins to wilt, tossing to combine. Transfer the vegetables to a serving platter and sprinkle with the coriander to garnish. Serve immediately.

1

2

Nutritional value per serve Fat: 10.1 g Carbohydrate: 12.3 g Protein: 4.7 g

Wilted rocket cheese salad

Preparation time 10 minutes Cooking time 10 minutes

Ingredients

- 3 tablespoons olive oil
- 4 slices white bread, crusts removed and cut into cubes
- 3 spring onions, sliced diagonally
- 2 cloves garlic, crushed
- 2 zucchini (courgettes), cut lengthwise into thin strips
- 1 red capsicum (pepper), thinly sliced
- 90 g (3 oz) raisins
- 2 bunches (about 250 g, 8 oz) rocket
- 125 g (4 oz) blue cheese, crumbled
- 2 tablespoons balsamic vinegar

serves 4

1 Heat 2 tablespoons oil in a wok over a medium heat. Add bread cubes and stir-fry for 3 minutes or until golden. Drain on absorbent kitchen paper. Heat remaining oil in wok, add spring onions and garlic and stir-fry for 2 minutes. Add zucchini, capsicum and raisins and stir-fry for 3 minutes or until vegetables are tender. Remove from wok, set aside.

2 Add rocket to the wok and stir-fry for 2 minutes or until rocket just wilts. Place rocket on a serving platter or divide between individual bowls or plates, top with vegetable mixture and scatter with croutons and blue cheese. Drizzle with balsamic vinegar and serve immediately.

1

2

Nutritional value per serve Fat: 13.8 g Carbohydrate: 11.4 g Protein: 5.7 g

Tomato, mustard and brie tart

Preparation time 25 minutes, plus 30 minutes refrigeration Cooking time 50 minutes

Ingredients

185 g (6 oz) plain flour
pinch of sea salt
90 g (3 oz) butter, diced
½ cup (125 ml, 4 fl oz) milk
2 egg yolks
1 clove garlic, crushed
1 tablespoon wholegrain mustard
60 g (2 oz) mature cheddar cheese, grated
4 tomatoes, sliced
125 g (4 oz) brie, thinly sliced
sea salt and freshly ground black pepper

Herb oil

1 tablespoon finely chopped fresh basil
1 tablespoon finely chopped fresh parsley
1 tablespoon finely chopped fresh coriander
2 tablespoons extra virgin olive oil

serves 4

1 Preheat oven to 190°C (375°F, gas mark 5). Sift flour and a pinch of sea salt into a large bowl. Using your fingertips, rub butter into flour until it resembles fine breadcrumbs. Add 2 tablespoons of cold water and mix to dough. Cover and refrigerate for 20 minutes. Roll pastry to line a deep 20 cm (8-in.) metal flan tin. Chill for a further 10 minutes.

2 Line pastry with baking paper and baking beans, bake blind for 10–12 minutes. Carefully remove paper and beans. Bake pastry for a further 5 minutes and set aside. Reduce oven temperature to 180°C (350°F, gas mark 4).

3 In a jug, place milk, egg yolks, garlic and seasoning. Whisk to combine. Spread mustard over pastry base and sprinkle with cheddar. Arrange tomatoes and brie on top, pour over egg mixture. Cook for 30–35 minutes, until just set and golden. In a small bowl, combine remaining ingredients and drizzle over tart. Serve warm.

1

2

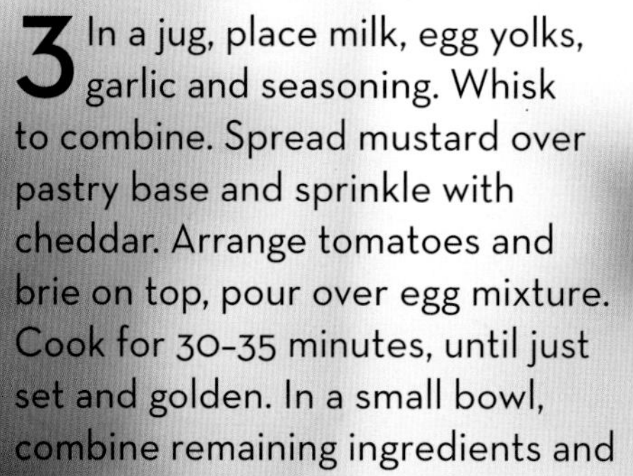
3

Nutritional value per serve Fat: 5.1 g Carbohydrate: 4.3 g Protein: 3.2 g

Mixed vegetable cheese bake

Preparation time 30 minutes Cooking time 1 hour 15 minutes

Ingredients

- 1 large butternut pumpkin, cut into chunks
- salt and black pepper
- 3 tablespoons olive oil
- 1 large (about 800 g, 1 lb 10 oz) cauliflower, cut into florets
- 360 g (12 oz) mushrooms, sliced
- 2 tablespoons fresh white breadcrumbs
- 2 tablespoons grated parmesan cheese

Sauce

- 2 tablespoons butter
- 30 g (1 oz) plain flour
- pinch of cayenne pepper
- 300 ml (10 fl oz) milk
- 1 teaspoon english mustard
- 100 g (3½ oz) cheddar cheese, grated
- extra butter for greasing
- black pepper

serves 4

1 Preheat oven to 200°C (400°F, gas mark 6). Place pumpkin into an ovenproof dish, season, drizzle with half the oil. Roast for 25 minutes, stirring once, until tender. Cook cauliflower in a large pan of boiling water for 5 minutes, until just tender. Drain, reserving 220 ml (7½ fl oz) of the cooking water, refresh in cold water and set aside. Heat remaining oil in a large frying pan. Cook mushrooms on a medium-high heat until just tender, tossing gently.

2 Melt butter in a large pan, stir in flour and cayenne pepper. Cook on a medium-low heat for 2 minutes, gradually stir in reserved cooking liquid. Cook for 2–3 minutes, until thick, gradually stir in the milk. Simmer, stirring, for 10 minutes. Remove from heat, stir in mustard and cheese, until melted. Season to taste.

3 Reduce oven temperature to 180°C (350°F, gas mark 4). Add cauliflower to pumpkin, toss gently to combine. Divide between four individual ovenproof dishes, top with mushrooms and pour over sauce. Combine breadcrumbs and parmesan, and sprinkle over each dish. Bake for 30–35 minutes.

2

3

Nutritional value per serve Fat: 3.1 g Carbohydrate: 6.6 g Protein: 4.5 g

Bean, lentil and eggplant moussaka

Preparation time 30 minutes Cooking time 1 hour 30 minutes

Ingredients

- 90 g (3 oz) lentils, rinsed and drained
- 1 eggplant (aubergine), thinly sliced
- 2 tablespoons olive oil
- 2 leeks, sliced
- 2 sticks celery, chopped
- 2 cloves garlic, crushed
- 1 yellow capsicum (pepper), diced
- 400 g (13 oz) can tomatoes, chopped
- ½ cup (125 ml, 4 fl oz) dry white wine
- 2 tablespoons tomato purée
- 400 g (13 oz) can black-eye (or other dried) beans, drained and rinsed
- 2 teaspoons dried mixed herbs
- black pepper
- 300 g (10 oz) low-fat natural yoghurt
- 2 eggs
- 4 tablespoons grated parmesan cheese
- fresh herbs to garnish

serves 4

1 Add lentils to a large pan of boiling water, cover, reduce heat and simmer for 30 minutes, until tender. Drain lentils, rinse, drain again and set aside.

2 Preheat oven to 180°C (350°F, gas mark 4). Cook eggplant slices in a pan of boiling water for 2 minutes. Drain, pat dry and set aside.

3 Heat oil in a large frying pan, add leeks, celery, garlic and capsicum and cook on a medium-high heat for 5 minutes, until softened. Add cooked lentils, tomatoes, wine, tomato purée, beans, mixed herbs and black pepper. Stir to combine, cover and bring to the boil. Reduce heat and simmer for 10 minutes, until vegetables have softened.

4 Spoon half the bean and lentil mixture into a shallow ovenproof dish and layer top with half the eggplant. Repeat. Combine yoghurt and eggs, and pour over the top. Sprinkle with parmesan. Cook for 40 minutes, until golden and bubbling. Garnish with fresh herbs.

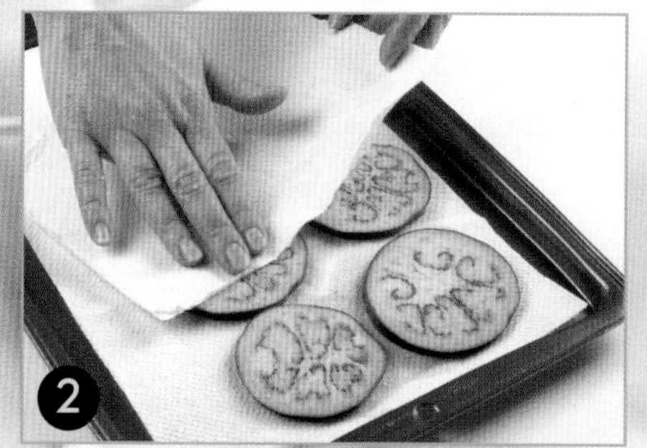

Nutritional value per serve Fat: 3 g Carbohydrate: 23 g Protein: 5.9 g

Linguine with leeks and mushrooms

Preparation time 20 minutes Cooking time 30 minutes

Ingredients
500 g (1 lb) leeks, sliced
290 g (10 oz) button mushrooms, sliced
1 bay leaf
3 tablespoons butter
45 g (1½ oz) plain flour
2 cups (500 ml, 16 fl oz) low-fat milk
2 tablespoons snipped fresh chives
extra chives to garnish
black pepper
500 g (1 lb) fresh linguine or tagliatelle
serves 4

1 Steam leeks, mushrooms and bay leaf over a large pan of boiling water for 10–15 minutes until tender. Discard bay leaf and keep the vegetables warm.

2 Melt butter in a large pan, add flour and cook gently for 1 minute, stirring. Remove from heat and gradually add milk. Return to heat and bring to the boil, stirring, until thickened. Reduce heat and simmer for 2 minutes, stirring. Add leek and mushrooms, chives and black pepper, heat through.

3 Cook pasta in a large pan of boiling water until al dente. Drain well, return to pan, add leek and mushroom sauce and toss lightly to combine. Garnish with fresh chives.

1

2

Nutritional value per serve Fat: 10 g Carbohydrate: 0.8 g Protein: 8 g

Asparagus, ricotta and herb frittata

Preparation time 20 minutes Cooking time 30–35 minutes

Ingredients

- 500 g (1 lb) fresh asparagus
- 12 eggs
- 2 cloves garlic, crushed
- 4 tablespoons chopped fresh mixed herbs (basil, chives, parsley etc)
- salt and black pepper
- 4 tablespoons butter
- 100 g (3½ oz) ricotta
- squeeze of lemon juice
- olive or truffle oil to drizzle
- parmesan cheese to serve
- extra whole chives to garnish

serves 4

1 Preheat grill to high. Char-grill asparagus on a griddle pan, until cooked and browned. Set aside and keep warm.

2 In a large bowl, whisk together eggs, garlic, herbs and seasoning. Melt half of the butter in an ovenproof frying pan, immediately pour in a quarter of the egg mixture and cook for 1–2 minutes, until almost set.

3 Place under preheated grill for 3–4 minutes, until egg is cooked through and top of frittata is set, transfer to a plate. Keep warm whilst making remaining frittatas, adding more butter when necessary.

4 Place frittatas on 4 serving plates and arrange a quarter of asparagus and a quarter of ricotta over each frittata. Squeeze over lemon juice, season and drizzle with oil. Top with shavings of parmesan and garnish with fresh chives.

Nutritional value per serve Fat: 4.7 g Carbohydrate: 15.2 g Protein: 3.6 g

Cajun barbecue corn

Preparation time 15 minutes Cooking time 25 minutes

Ingredients

- 4 cobs sweetcorn, halved
- 1 orange sweet potato, cut into 1 cm thick slices
- 2 tablespoons butter, melted

Cajun spice mix

- 1 teaspoon freshly ground black pepper
- ½ teaspoon chilli powder
- 1 teaspoon ground cumin
- 1 teaspoon ground coriander
- 2 teaspoons sweet paprika

serves 4

1 Preheat barbecue to high heat.

2 In a small bowl, place black pepper, chilli powder, cumin, coriander and paprika and mix to combine.

3 Brush sweetcorn and sweet potato with butter, sprinkle spice mix over vegetables.

4 Place sweetcorn and sweet potato on barbecue and cook, turning frequently, for 10–15 minutes or until vegetables are cooked.

2

3

4

Nutritional value per serve Fat: 14.1 g Carbohydrate: 8.5 g Protein: 2 g

Potato and onion dauphinoise

Preparation time 20 minutes Cooking time 1 hour

Ingredients

1 tablespoon butter

extra butter for greasing

750 g (1½ lb) baking potatoes, thinly sliced

3 onions, thinly sliced

1 teaspoon freshly grated nutmeg

450 ml (14 fl oz) thickened cream

salt and black pepper

serves 2–4

1 Preheat oven to 180°C (350°F, gas mark 4). Grease a shallow ovenproof dish with butter.

2 Arrange potatoes and onions in alternate layers in baking dish. Lightly season each layer with salt, pepper and nutmeg. Finish with a potato layer, pour over cream and dot with butter. Place on lower shelf of oven and cook for 1 hour until golden.

Nutritional value per serve Fat: 22.1 g Carbohydrate: 2.6 g Protein: 4.5 g

Broccoli soufflés with olive purée

Preparation time 15 minutes Cooking time 40 minutes

Ingredients

butter for greasing

450 g (14 oz) broccoli, chopped

280 ml (9 fl oz) thickened cream

4 medium eggs, separated

salt and black pepper

Olive purée

20 pitted black olives

1/2 cup (125 ml, 4 fl oz) olive oil

grated rind (zest) and juice of 1 lemon

serves 4

1 Preheat oven to 220°C (425°F, gas mark 7). Grease 4 individual 1 cup (250 ml, 8 fl oz) capacity ramekin dishes. Cook broccoli in a little boiling water for 10 minutes until tender, drain well. Process to a smooth purée with the cream, egg yolks and seasoning in a food processor. Transfer to a large mixing bowl.

1

2 Beat egg whites to form soft peaks. Gently fold one-third of the beaten whites into the broccoli purée, using a large metal spoon. Carefully fold in the remaining whites in two batches, mixing well.

2

3 Divide mixture between ramekin dishes and cook for 20–25 minutes, until risen and golden. Purée olives, olive oil and lemon rind (zest) and juice in a food processor until smooth. Serve with warm soufflés and crusty bread.

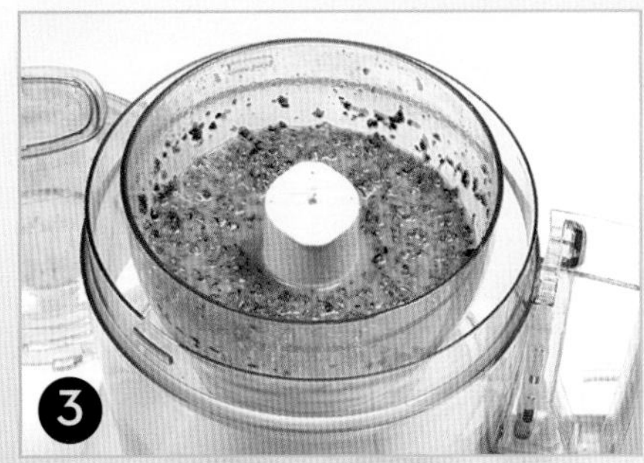

3

Nutritional value per serve Fat: 7.8 g Carbohydrate: 1.3 g Protein: 2.9 g

Mushrooms in wine

Preparation time 10 minutes Cooking time 25 minutes

Ingredients
4 tablespoons olive oil
1 small clove garlic, peeled
750 g (1 1/2 lb) mushrooms, sliced
1 tablespoon chopped fresh thyme
salt
freshly ground black pepper
1/2 cup (125 ml, 4 fl oz) white wine
2 tablespoons chopped fresh parsley
serves 4–6

1 Heat oil and garlic in a large pan over high heat, add mushrooms and thyme and cook, stirring, for 1–2 minutes. Season to taste, add wine and bring to the boil. Boil rapidly until wine is almost evaporated. Transfer to a serving bowl, sprinkle with parsley and serve hot or cold.

Nutritional value per serve Fat: 21.9 g Carbohydrate: 19 g Protein: 4.4 g

Red onion and chilli tarts

Preparation time 15 minutes Cooking time 25 minutes

Ingredients
4 sheets (370 g, 12 oz) ready-rolled puff pastry
1 tablespoon olive oil
200 g (7 oz) red onions, finely sliced lengthways
1 small red chilli, deseeded and sliced
salt and black pepper
2 tablespoons sun-dried tomato pesto
3 tablespoons pine nuts
makes 4

1 Preheat oven to 220°C (425°F, gas mark 7). Cut 4 x 12 cm (5-in.) rounds of pastry. Score a 1 cm (½-in.) border on each – to form a rim. Place the rounds on a greased baking sheet.

2 Heat oil in a large frying pan. Cook onions on a medium-high heat for 10 minutes, until softened, stirring. Add chilli, cook gently for 1 minute, and season.

3 Spread pesto over the pastry rounds, leaving the rim clear. Spoon onion mixture over the pesto and sprinkle with pine nuts. Bake in the oven for 12–15 minutes until golden.

Nutritional value per serve Fat: 4.9 g Carbohydrate: 3.2 g Protein: 1.5 g

Eggplant and bean with basil

Preparation time 5 minutes, plus 20 minutes resting Cooking time 18 minutes

Ingredients

- 3 eggplants (aubergines), halved lengthways and cut into $^1/_2$ cm ($^1/_4$-in.) thick slices
- salt
- 1 tablespoon vegetable oil
- 2 onions, cut into thin wedges, layers separated
- 3 fresh red chillies, chopped
- 2 cloves garlic, sliced
- 1 stalk fresh lemongrass, chopped
- 250 g (8 oz) green beans, trimmed
- 1 cup (250 ml, 8 fl oz) coconut milk
- 45 g (1$^1/_2$ oz) basil leaves

serves 6

1 Place eggplants in a colander, sprinkle with salt and set aside for 20 minutes. Rinse under cold running water and pat dry on absorbent kitchen paper.

2 Heat oil in a wok or frying pan over a high heat. Add onions, chillies, garlic and lemongrass and stir-fry for 3 minutes. Add eggplants, beans and coconut milk and heat until almost boiling. Turn down heat, cover and simmer for 15 minutes until eggplants are tender. Stir in basil and serve immediately.

Nutritional value per serve Fat: 5.9 g Carbohydrate: 12 g Protein: 6.2 g

Vegetarian lasagne

Preparation time 30 minutes Cooking time 1 hour, plus 10 minutes standing

Ingredients

- 250 g (8 oz) instant lasagne sheets
- 200 g (7 oz) ricotta cheese
- 250 g (8 oz) mozzarella cheese, grated
- 2 tablespoons oil
- 1 large eggplant (aubergine)
- 125 g (4 oz) mushrooms, sliced
- 1 carrot, grated
- 1 zucchini (courgette), grated
- 500 g (1 lb) jar pasta sauce
- 140 g (4½ oz) tomato paste
- 1 cup (250 ml, 8 fl oz) water
- ½ cup (125 ml, 4 fl oz) red wine
- 2 tablespoons chopped fresh parsley

serves 4–6

1 Preheat oven to 190°C (375°F, gas mark 5). In a large pan, heat oil, add eggplant, mushrooms, carrot and zucchini and cook on a medium-high heat for 2–3 minutes. Stir in pasta sauce, tomato paste, water, wine and parsley. Cover, reduce heat and simmer for 15 minutes, stirring occasionally.

2 Grease a 20 x 30 cm (8 x 12-in.) ovenproof dish with butter and spread ⅓ of vegetable sauce over base. Cover with a layer of lasagne sheets. Spread ⅓ of ricotta onto pasta and sprinkle with ⅓ cup mozzarella.

3 Repeat the layers twice, finishing with ricotta and sprinkling with cup of mozzarella.

4 Bake for 30–40 minutes, until golden and bubbling. Stand for 10 minutes before serving.

Nutritional value per serve Fat: 5.4 g Carbohydrate: 8.6 g Protein: 7 g

Baked ricotta mushrooms

Preparation time 15 minutes Cooking time 15 minutes

Ingredients

- 10 large mushrooms, stems removed
- 1 tablespoon parmesan cheese, grated
- 1 tablespoon dried breadcrumbs

Ricotta and herb filling

- 125 g (4 oz) ricotta cheese
- 3 sun-dried tomatoes, soaked in warm water until soft, chopped
- 1 tablespoon red onion, finely diced
- 1 tablespoon chopped fresh basil
- 1 tablespoon snipped fresh chives
- 1 teaspoon lemon juice
- freshly ground black pepper

makes 10

1 Preheat oven to 180°C (350°F, gas mark 4). Line a baking tray with non-stick baking paper. Set aside.

2 In a large bowl, place ricotta, tomatoes, onion, basil, chives, lemon juice and black pepper to taste. Mix to combine.

3 Spoon filling into mushroom caps and place on prepared baking tray. Combine parmesan and breadcrumbs. Sprinkle over mushrooms. Bake for 10–15 minutes or until filling is set and top is golden.

2

3

Chicken and seafood are key sources of protein. They can be prepared quickly in a variety of different ways – home-made fast food! Purchase them whole or in pieces and cuts. There's no waste with either food and, if you remove the skin from chicken, very little fat.

These recipes draw on an exciting range of influences, including Asia and Europe, as well as more traditional sources. Their diversity means that there's a wide range of dishes to choose from, whatever the occasion.

Other recipes based on chicken and seafood can also be found in the sections on Starters and Pasta, Rice and Noodles.

Purchasing and storage tips for chicken

Make fresh chicken, whole or in pieces, your last purchase when shopping. If possible, place the chicken in an insulated bag to keep it cold on the trip home.

Immediately on arrival home, remove the chicken from its package, rinse it and pat it dry. Place in a dish and cover loosely with plastic wrap. Place the dish in the coldest part of the refrigerator, below 4°C (30°F). Cook the chicken within 3 days.

When buying frozen chicken, make sure it is frozen solid. Check that there are no signs of a torn package or ice deposits in the base of the package, as these are signs of a partial thaw.

Place the frozen chicken in the freezer immediately on arrival home. For health and taste, frozen chicken must be thoroughly thawed before cooking. Do not refreeze thawed chicken in its raw state.

Thaw frozen chicken in the refrigerator (not on the kitchen bench). Place it on a rack in a dish and cover it loosely with plastic wrap. Allow the chicken to thaw completely before cooking. Chicken can also be thawed in a microwave, following manufacturer's directions.

Cuts of chicken

Breast fillets are very tender, but will toughen if overcooked. Cook them quickly, whatever the method. Thicker pieces of chicken such as Maryland, half-breasts, drumsticks and thighs need a lower heat and longer cooking time. Move them closer to the source of heat towards the end to crisp and brown them.

Breast fillets: If pan frying, make breast fillets an even thickness to ensure good contact with the pan. Place the fillets between two sheets of plastic wrap and lightly pound them with a meat mallet or a rolling pin until thickness is evened out.

Thigh fillets: Thigh fillets have had the bone and skin removed, making them ideal for pan frying, schnitzels and, when pounded thinly, forming into rolls with stuffing.

Chicken wings: Wings may be cooked whole or with the joints separated. For whole wings, turn the wing up behind the end joint to form a triangular shape.

Nutritional value per serve Fat: 14.9 g Carbohydrate: 4 g Protein: 10.5 g

Chicken laksa

Preparation time 20 minutes Cooking time 32 minutes

Ingredients

$^{1}/_{3}$ cup (90 ml, 3 fl oz) vegetable oil

4 small fresh red chillies, finely chopped

1 stalk fresh lemongrass, finely chopped or $^{1}/_{2}$ teaspoon dried lemongrass, soaked in hot water until soft

3 cloves garlic, crushed

2 tablespoons finely grated fresh ginger

1 teaspoon ground cumin

1 teaspoon ground turmeric

6 candlenuts or unsalted macadamia nuts

$^{1}/_{4}$ teaspoon shrimp paste

1 litre ($1^{2}/_{3}$ pints) coconut milk

4 boneless chicken breast fillets, cut into 2 cm ($^{3}/_{4}$-in.) cubes

2 tablespoons chopped fresh coriander

375 g (12 oz) rice noodles, cooked

125 g (4 oz) bean sprouts

125 g (4 oz) fried tofu, sliced

serves 4

1 Into a food processor place 2 tablespoons oil, chillies, lemongrass, garlic, ginger, cumin, turmeric, candlenuts or macadamia nuts and shrimp paste and process to make a smooth paste.

2 In a large saucepan, heat the remaining oil over a medium heat, add paste and cook, stirring, for 2 minutes or until fragrant. Stir in coconut milk and simmer, stirring occasionally, for 15 minutes or until mixture thickens slightly.

3 Add chicken and coriander and simmer, stirring occasionally, for 15 minutes longer or until chicken is tender. To serve, divide rice noodles between serving bowls, top with bean sprouts and tofu and pour over coconut milk mixture.

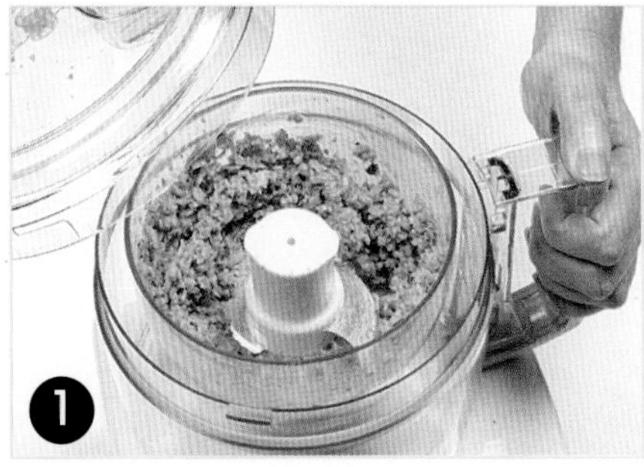
1

2

3

Nutritional value per serve Fat: 11.5 g Carbohydrate: 7.5 g Protein: 10.8 g

Chicken and leek soup with herb dumplings

Preparation time 25 minutes Cooking time 2 hours

Ingredients

- 4 chicken thighs on the bone, about 800 g (1 lb 10 oz)
- 1 onion, chopped
- 1 carrot, chopped
- herb bundle made up of fresh tarragon, parsley and a bay leaf
- 4 tablespoons butter
- 300 g (10 oz) potatoes, cubed
- 3 large leeks, sliced
- salt and black pepper
- 2 chicken breast fillets, about 500 g (1 lb), cut into small strips
- 2 teaspoons chopped fresh tarragon
- 150 ml (5 fl oz) thickened cream

Dumplings

- 100 g (3½ oz) self-raising flour
- 30 g (1 oz) fresh white breadcrumbs
- 60 g (2 oz) shredded suet
- 3 tablespoons chopped fresh herbs (tarragon, parsley or chives)

serves 4

1 Place the chicken thighs, onion, carrot and herbs in a large pan with 1.5 litres (2½ pints) of water. Simmer, covered, for 1 hour. Strain the stock and skim off any fat. Finely chop the chicken, discarding the skin and bones. Heat half the butter in a separate large pan. Add the potatoes and ⅔ of the leeks, cover and cook for 10 minutes. Pour in 1 litre (1⅔ pints) of the stock and season. Simmer for 10–15 minutes, until softened. Blend until smooth in a food processor, return to the pan, then stir in the cooked chicken. Set aside, keep warm.

2 To make the dumplings, combine flour, breadcrumbs, suet, herbs and seasoning in a large bowl. Stir in 4 tablespoons of water, mix well to combine, then shape into 8 dumplings. Cook in simmering salted water for 15–20 minutes.

3 Heat the remaining butter in a large frying pan. Cook the chicken breast strips for 4–5 minutes or until done. Add the remaining leek and cook for 2–3 minutes, until tender, then add to the soup with the tarragon and more stock, if necessary. Bring to the boil and simmer for 2 minutes. Remove from the heat and stir in the cream. Divide between 4 serving bowls. Drain the dumplings and add 2 to each bowl.

Nutritional value per serve Fat: 9.3 g Carbohydrate: 11.2 g Protein: 13.4 g

Chicken and prune roll

Preparation time 20 minutes Cooking time 40 minutes

Ingredients

- 2 rashers of bacon, finely chopped
- 1 medium onion, finely chopped
- 5 pitted prunes, chopped
- 500 g (1 lb) chicken mince
- 2 tablespoons dried breadcrumbs
- ½ teaspoon salt
- ½ teaspoon pepper
- 1 teaspoon cumin
- 1 egg, lightly beaten
- 1 sheet frozen puff pastry
- 5 pitted whole prunes
- 1 tablespoon milk
- 2 teaspoons poppy seeds

serves 6–8

1 In a small heated pan, place bacon and onion and cook while stirring for 1 minute. Mix the chopped prunes, chicken mince, breadcrumbs, salt, pepper, cumin, egg, and the bacon and onion mixture. Combine well.

2 Preheat the oven to 200°C (400°F, gas mark 6). Line a flat oven tray with a sheet of baking paper and place a sheet of thawed puff pastry onto the tray. Spoon ½ of the mince mixture along the centre of the sheet in an even strip about 8 cm (3-in.) wide and to the edge of the pastry at both ends. Arrange the 5 whole prunes along the centre then cover with remaining mince and smooth to even thickness.

3 Brush the back strip of pastry with water, lift the front pastry over the mince and lift the back pastry to overlap the front. Press lightly along the seam to seal. Lift paper and turn the chicken roll over to rest on the seam join. Pull paper to bring it into the centre of the tray, trim off paper overhang. Glaze roll with milk and sprinkle with poppy seeds.

4 Bake in the oven for 15 minutes. Turn oven down to 180°C (350°F, gas mark 4) and continue cooking for 25 minutes until golden. Slice and serve with salad garnish.

Nutritional value per serve Fat: 4.9 g Carbohydrate: 1 g Protein: 16.6 g

Chicken rogan josh

Preparation time 15 minutes Cooking time 45 minutes

Ingredients

- 1 tablespoon vegetable oil
- 1 small green capsicum (pepper), thinly sliced
- 1 small red capsicum (pepper), thinly sliced
- 1 onion, thinly sliced
- 5 cm (2-in.) piece of fresh root ginger, finely chopped
- 2 cloves garlic, crushed
- 2 tablespoons garam masala
- 1 teaspoon paprika
- 1 teaspoon turmeric
- 1 teaspoon chilli powder
- 4 cardamom pods, crushed
- salt to taste
- 8 chicken thigh fillets, each cut into 4 pieces
- 200 g (7 oz) natural yoghurt
- 400 g (13 oz) can chopped tomatoes
- 200 ml (7 fl oz) water
- fresh coriander to garnish
- mango chutney to serve
- steamed rice to serve

serves 4

1 Heat the oil in a heavy-based frying pan. Add the capsicums, onion, ginger, garlic, spices and salt. Cover and fry over a low heat for 5 minutes or until the capsicums and onion have softened.

2 Add the chicken and stir until it changes colour. Stir in the yoghurt and cook gently for 5 minutes.

3 Stir in the tomatoes and water and bring to the boil. Reduce the heat, cover, and simmer for 30 minutes or until the chicken is tender, stirring occasionally and adding more water if the sauce becomes too dry. Sprinkle with coriander. Serve with steamed rice and mango chutney.

Nutritional value per serve Fat: 5.5 g Carbohydrate: 3.2 g Protein: 13.4 g

Hawaiian poached chicken

Preparation time 15 minutes Cooking time 40 minutes

Ingredients

- 1½ kg (3 lb) chicken casserole pieces
- ½ teaspoon salt
- ½ teaspoon pepper
- 1 teaspoon paprika
- 2 tablespoons oil
- 1 large onion, chopped
- 1 clove garlic, crushed
- 4 tablespoons water
- 1 tablespoon worcestershire sauce
- 2 teaspoons sweet chilli sauce
- 4 tablespoons apple cider vinegar
- 1½ tablespoons brown sugar
- ½ medium fresh pineapple, peeled and diced
- 1 green capsicum (pepper), seeded and cut into thin strips
- 1 red capsicum (pepper), seeded and cut into thin strips
- 1 tablespoon rum (optional)
- 1½ tablespoons cornflour
- boiled rice to serve

serves 6

1 Season the chicken pieces with salt, pepper and paprika. Heat the oil in a large saucepan. Add chicken pieces a few at a time and brown on all sides. Remove to a plate lined with kitchen paper as they brown. Drain the oil from the saucepan.

2 Add the onion and garlic to the saucepan and cook, stirring for 2 minutes. Return chicken to the saucepan. In a bowl, combine the water, worcestershire sauce, sweet chilli sauce, vinegar and brown sugar and pour over the chicken. Add the pineapple pieces and capsicums. Simmer for 30–35 minutes until chicken is tender.

3 Add the rum to the chicken. Blend the cornflour and water together. Add the cornflour mixture to the chicken and stir through. Allow to simmer until sauce thickens. Increase the heat until it boils then turn off heat. Serve with boiled rice.

Nutritional value per serve Fat: 9.9 g Carbohydrate: 2.6 g Protein: 20 g

Oven-baked parmesan chicken

Preparation time 15 minutes Cooking time 20 minutes

Ingredients

- 60 g (2 oz) fresh breadcrumbs, made from country-style bread
- 75 g (3 oz) parmesan, finely grated
- 2 spring onions, finely chopped
- finely grated rind (zest) and juice of 1/2 lemon
- 4 tablespoons butter, melted
- sea salt and freshly ground black pepper
- 4 chicken breast fillets
- 2 tablespoons chopped fresh parsley

serves 4

1 Preheat the oven to 190°C (375°F, gas mark 5). In a small bowl, mix together the breadcrumbs, parmesan, spring onions, lemon rind, butter, salt and pepper.

2 Divide the mixture between the chicken breasts and using a fork or your hands, press the mixture on top, to form an even coat.

3 Transfer the chicken breasts to a greased shallow oven tray and bake for 20 minutes. Remove the chicken and keep warm. Add the lemon juice and parsley to the buttery juices in the tray and mix well. Pour these juices over the chicken and serve immediately.

Nutritional value per serve Fat: 10.9 g Carbohydrate: 13.3 g Protein: 11.9 g

Mustard and honey chicken drumsticks with mustard cream sauce

Preparation time 30 minutes, plus 30 minutes marinating

Cooking time 35–40 minutes

Ingredients

2¼ kg (4.5 lb) chicken drumsticks

Mustard cream sauce

1¼ cups (315 ml, 10 fl oz) sour cream

1 cup (250 ml, 8 fl oz) dijon mustard

½ cup (125 ml, 4 fl oz) honey and chilli marinade

Honey and chilli marinade

¾ cup (185 ml, 6 fl oz) red wine

1½ cups (375 ml, 12 fl oz) honey

¾ teaspoon ground chilli

3 teaspoons mustard powder

serves 6–10

1 In a large bowl, combine red wine, honey, chilli and mustard powder. Set aside and reserve ½ cup (125 ml, 4 fl oz) marinade in a separate bowl. Place drumsticks in a large glass dish and pour over 1¾ cups (435 ml, 14 fl oz) marinade. Cover and stand 30 minutes at room temperature or overnight in the refrigerator.

2 Heat a flat-top, charcoal or gas barbecue until hot. Lightly oil grill bars, place drumsticks on barbecue and cook for 30–35 minutes or until golden and cooked through to the bone. Brush frequently with marinade and turn drumsticks to brown evenly. (They can be cooked in a kettle/weber for 40–45 minutes.)

3 In a heat-proof bowl, combine sour cream, mustard, and remaining ½ cup (125 ml, 4 fl oz) honey and chilli marinade. Place at the side of the barbecue to heat through. Serve drumsticks with the mustard cream sauce.

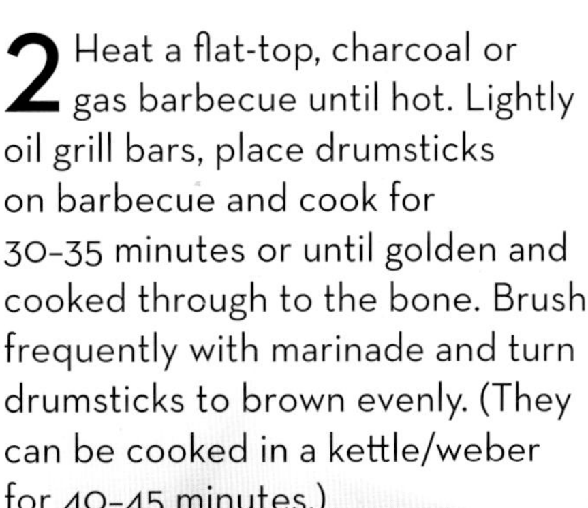

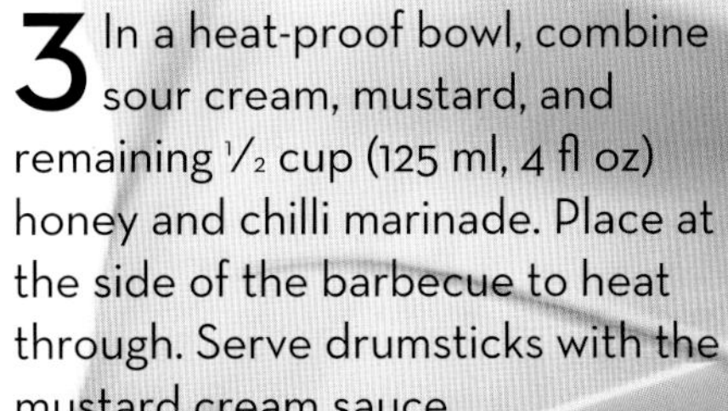

Nutritional value per serve Fat: 15.3 g Carbohydrate: 20 g Protein: 12.8 g

Chicken and mushroom linguine

Preparation time 20 minutes Cooking time 30 minutes

Ingredients

1 tablespoon sunflower oil
500 g (1 lb) chicken breast fillet, cut into 4 portions
6 cloves garlic, unpeeled
250 g (8 oz) brown cap mushrooms or wild mushrooms
220 ml (7½ fl oz) thickened cream
salt and black pepper
500 g (1 lb) fresh linguine
3 tablespoons butter
125 g (4 oz) parmesan cheese, grated
serves 4

1 Preheat oven to 200°C (400°F, gas mark 6). Heat oil in a large frying pan, add chicken and fry for 1 minute on each side, until browned. Place chicken in an ovenproof dish.

2 Add garlic cloves to the pan, fry for 3 minutes until softened. Remove from pan, leave to cool slightly, peel, mash and add to chicken with mushrooms, cream and seasoning. Cover dish with foil and bake for 20 minutes.

3 Cook pasta in a large pan of boiling water, until al dente. Drain, return to the pan, toss with butter and parmesan. Serve linguine topped with chicken and mushroom mixture.

1

2

3

Nutritional value per serve Fat: 8.7 g Carbohydrate: 4.6 g Protein: 11.9 g

Chicken and leek flan with almond topping

Preparation time 15 minutes Cooking time 1 hour

Ingredients

- 2 frozen savoury 20 cm (8-in.) flan cases
- 1 tablespoon canola oil
- 2 leeks, trimmed, washed and thinly sliced
- 500 g (1 lb) chicken breast fillets, sliced into 1 cm (1/2-in.) slices
- 200 g (7 oz) button mushrooms, sliced
- 1 tablespoon lemon juice
- 1 cup (250 ml, 8 fl oz) water
- 1 cup (250 ml, 8 fl oz) milk
- 45 g (1 1/2 oz) packet cream of chicken soup mix
- 2 eggs, lightly beaten
- 1/4 teaspoon nutmeg
- 100 g (3 1/2 oz) flaked almonds

serves 4–6 per flan

1 Preheat oven to 180°C (350°F, gas mark 4). Place frozen flan cases on a tray in the oven. Blind bake for 10–15 minutes. Remove and set aside.

2 Heat oil in a large saucepan and cook leeks for 5 minutes until soft. Remove to a bowl. Add the chicken pieces to saucepan and cook for 1 minute on each side. Add mushrooms and lemon juice, turn down heat and simmer for 3 minutes. Return the leeks to the saucepan and set aside.

3 In a saucepan, combine water and milk and stir in the soup mix. Place over heat and bring to the boil while stirring. Cook until thick. Pour into the chicken mixture and stir to combine. Allow the mixture to cool a little before stirring in the eggs and nutmeg.

4 Remove blind bake from flan cases and fill with chicken filling. Sprinkle flaked almonds to make a dense covering. Bake for 25–30 minutes until filling is set.

1

3

4

Nutritional value per serve Fat: 7.7 g Carbohydrate: 6.6 g Protein: 15.7 g

Easy apricot and mango chicken loaf

Preparation time 8 minutes Cooking time 55 minutes, plus 10 minutes standing

Ingredients

- 700 g (1 lb 7 oz) chicken mince
- 60 g (2 oz) fresh breadcrumbs
- 90 g (3 oz) spring onions, chopped including green part
- 1 tablespoon finely chopped parsley
- 2 tablespoons diced dried apricots
- 1 tablespoon mango chutney
- 1 egg
- 1 teaspoon salt
- ¼ teaspoon pepper
- oil for greasing

serves 6

1 Preheat oven to 180°C (350°F, gas mark 4). In a large bowl, place chicken mince. Add breadcrumbs, spring onions, parsley, apricots, chutney, egg, salt and pepper. With your hand, mix and knead mixture for 2–3 minutes to combine ingredients well and to give a fine texture.

2 Grease a 22 x 8 x 5 cm (8 x 3 x 2-in.) loaf tin with oil and add the mince mixture. Place in oven and bake for 50–55 minutes. To test insert skewer into centre and if clear juice appears loaf is cooked. If juice is a pink colour further cooking is required. Rest loaf in the tin 10 minutes before turning out.

1

2

Nutritional value per serve Fat: 8.9 g Carbohydrate: 0.9 g Protein: 13.8 g

Warm thai chicken salad

Preparation time 15 minutes, plus 20 minutes standing Cooking time 15 minutes

Ingredients

4 chicken breast fillets

2 teaspoons ready-made thai-style marinade

1 teaspoon oil

1 red capsicum (pepper), deseeded and cut into strips

1 green capsicum (pepper), deseeded and cut into strips

1 eggplant (aubergine), sliced

1 spanish onion, cut into rings

½ cos (romaine) lettuce, shredded

Dressing

½ cup (125 ml, 4 fl oz) olive oil

4 tablespoons malt vinegar

extra teaspoon ready-made thai-style marinade

serves 4

1 Flatten chicken breasts slightly to even thickness. In a small bowl, combine 2 teaspoons thai-style marinade and 1 teaspoon oil and rub well into the chicken. Cover and stand 20 minutes before cooking.

2 Heat the barbecue to medium-high and lightly oil hotplate and grill bars. Place chicken on grill and cook 4 minutes each side. Place capsicum, eggplant and onion on the hotplate, drizzle with a little oil and cook for 5–8 minutes, tossing to cook through. Pile lettuce onto individual plates and place barbecued vegetables in the centre. Cut the chicken into thin diagonal slices and arrange on top of vegetables.

3 In a small bowl, combine vinegar and remaining oil and thai-style marinade and pour over chicken and warm salad. Serve with slices of crusty bread.

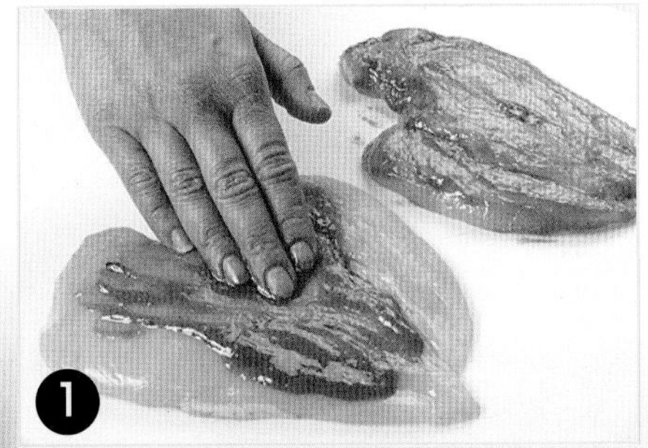
1

2

Nutritional value per serve Fat: 12.1 g Carbohydrate: 6.9 g Protein: 5.4 g

Hot chicken ball salad with fruity dressing

Preparation time 25 minutes Cooking time 15 minutes

Ingredients

- 500 g (1 lb) chicken mince
- 1/2 teaspoon salt
- 1/2 teaspoon pepper
- 2 tablespoons dried breadcrumbs
- 1 medium onion, very finely chopped
- 2 tablespoons finely chopped parsley
- 1 tablespoon lemon juice
- 1 egg
- 3 tablespoons flour for dusting
- oil for frying
- 500 g (1 lb) mixed salad greens

Fruity dressing

- 4 tablespoons apple cider vinegar
- 1 tablespoon mustard powder
- 1 tablespoon soy sauce
- 450 g (14 oz) can pineapple pieces
- 2 large bananas, sliced
- 2 tablespoons cornflour, blended with 2 tablespoons cold water

serves 6

1 In a bowl, combine the chicken mince with the salt, pepper, breadcrumbs, onion, parsley, lemon juice and egg. Knead for 2 minutes to mix and make a fine-grained mince. Take tablespoons of mince and roll them into balls with wet hands.

2 Heat enough oil to be about 1 cm (1/2-in.) deep in the frying pan. Roll the chicken balls in flour, shake off excess. Add a third of the balls and fry, rolling them around to cook all sides. Remove and drain on absorbent kitchen paper. Cook remainder.

3 In a saucepan, place vinegar, mustard and soy sauce. Add the juice from the pineapple pieces and blend in the cornflour. Stir over heat until the sauce thickens and boils. Add the pineapple pieces, bananas, chicken balls and heat through. Pile salad greens on individual plates or a platter and spoon on the chicken balls and sauce. Serve immediately.

1

3

Nutritional value per serve Fat: 6.3 g Carbohydrate: 4.5 g Protein: 6.2 g

Chicken waldorf

Preparation time 10 minutes Cooking time 20 minutes

Ingredients

400 g (13 oz) chicken breast fillets

1 onion, roughly chopped

1 carrot, roughly chopped

pinch of salt

2 red apples

1 tablespoon lemon juice

2 sticks celery, diced

60 g (2 oz) blonde walnuts, coarsely chopped

125 g (4 oz) mayonnaise

1 lettuce, separated into cups, washed and crisped

serves 6–8

1 To poach the chicken fillets: place fillets, onion, carrot and salt in a pan and add hot water just to cover. Bring to a simmer, reduce heat and simmer gently for 20 minutes. Turn off heat and cool in its juices. Strain, reserve stock for future use.

2 Cut chicken into 1 cm (1/2-in.) cubes. Wash apples well, leave skin on and cut into 1 cm (1/2-in.) cubes. Sprinkle with lemon juice.

3 In a bowl, toss chicken, apples, celery and walnuts together. Add mayonnaise and gently toss through. Spoon into the lettuce cups and serve as an entrée or light lunch; or line a salad bowl with lettuce leaves and pile salad into the centre and serve for a buffet.

Nutritional value per serve Fat: 5.9 g Carbohydrate: 13 g Protein: 3.7 g

Apricot chicken pilaf

Preparation time 10 minutes, plus 2 hours soaking Cooking time 45–50 minutes

Ingredients

- 1½ cups (300 g, 10 oz) long-grain rice water for soaking
- 1 teaspoon salt
- 1 kg (2 lb) chicken thigh fillets
- 3 tablespoons butter
- 1 large onion, finely chopped
- 45 g (1½ oz) pine nuts
- ½ teaspoon fresh thyme, chopped
- salt and freshly ground black pepper
- ¼ teaspoon ground cinnamon
- 3½ cups (875 ml, 28 fl oz) hot chicken stock
- 100 g (3½ oz) dried apricots, diced
- 100 g (3½ oz) seeded raisins

serves 6

1 Place rice in water to cover, add salt and soak for 2 hours. Drain thoroughly. Cut each thigh fillet into 3 or 4 pieces. Heat 2 tablespoons butter in a large, heavy-based saucepan and brown the chicken well on all sides over high heat. Remove to a plate.

2 Add remaining butter and sauté the onion and pine nuts. Add thyme, salt, pepper and cinnamon. Add the drained rice and stir to coat well with butter. Heat chicken stock to boiling and pour over the rice. Return chicken pieces to saucepan and stir in apricots and raisins. Bring back to the boil for 2 minutes, then lower the heat, cover the saucepan and simmer for 10 minutes.

3 Place a folded tea towel under the saucepan lid, pressing lid down tightly. Turn down heat to very low and cook for 30–35 minutes undisturbed. Fluff up rice with a fork and serve hot.

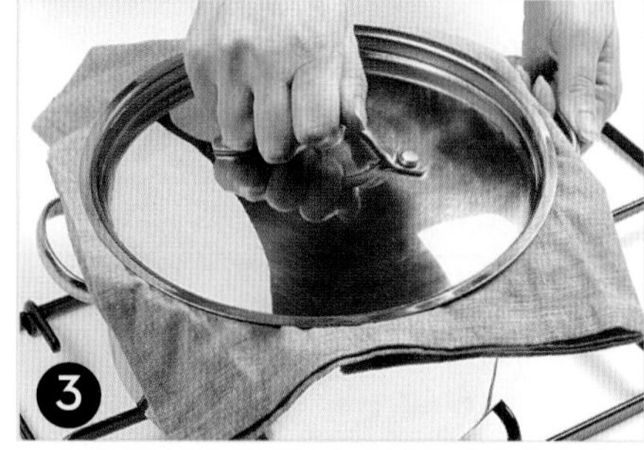

Nutritional value per serve Fat: 20.4 g Carbohydrate: 3.1 g Protein: 13.4 g

Smoked salmon soufflés

Preparation time 15 minutes Cooking time 35 minutes

Ingredients

- 45 g (1½ oz) parmesan cheese
- 1 tablespoon butter
- 2 tablespoons plain flour
- ½ cup (125 ml, 4 fl oz) milk
- 4 tablespoons thickened cream
- 3 eggs, separated
- 60 g (2 oz) gruyère cheese, grated
- 60 g (2 oz) smoked salmon, shredded
- 1 tablespoon chopped fresh dill

serves 2

1 Grease 2 ramekins of 1 cup (250 ml, 8 fl oz) capacity and sprinkle base and sides with 30 g (1 oz) parmesan cheese.

2 Melt butter in a small pan over a medium heat. Stir in flour and cook for 2 minutes. Remove pan from heat and gradually whisk in milk and cream.

3 Return pan to heat and cook, stirring constantly, for 4 minutes or until sauce boils and thickens. Remove pan from heat and set aside to cool slightly.

4 Add egg yolks, gruyère cheese, remaining parmesan cheese, salmon and dill to sauce and mix to combine.

5 In a large bowl, place egg whites and beat until stiff peaks form. Fold egg white mixture into salmon mixture. Pour into ramekins and bake for 20–25 minutes or until soufflés are puffed and golden. Serve immediately.

2

5

Nutritional value per serve Fat: 1.9 g Carbohydrate: 5.2 g Protein: 11.3 g

Lime fish with noodles

Preparation time 10 minutes Cooking time 5 minutes

Ingredients

- 2 teaspoons vegetable oil
- 3 spring onions, chopped
- 1 stalk fresh lemongrass, chopped or 1/2 teaspoon dried lemongrass, soaked in hot water until soft
- 1 fresh red chilli, chopped
- 750 g (1 1/2 lb) firm white fish fillets, cut into thick strips
- 2 tablespoons lime juice
- 315 g (10 oz) fresh rice noodles
- 1/2 bunch (250 g, 8 oz) bok choy (pak choi), chopped
- 4 tablespoons water
- 2 tablespoons soy sauce
- 2 teaspoons white miso

serves 4

1 Heat wok over a high heat, add the oil, spring onions, lemongrass and chilli and stir-fry for 1 minute. Add fish and lime juice and stir-fry for 2 minutes or until fish is almost cooked. Remove fish mixture from wok and set aside.

2 Add noodles, bok choy, water, soy sauce and miso to wok and stir-fry for 2 minutes. Return fish mixture to wok and stir-fry for 1 minute or until heated through.

Nutritional value per serve Fat: 11 g Carbohydrate: 8.5 g Protein: 13.7 g

Oriental-style salmon fillets

Preparation time 5 minutes, plus 30–60 minutes marinating Cooking time 8 minutes

Ingredients

- 4 skinless salmon fillets
- 2 tablespoons vegetable oil
- 2 tablespoons light soy sauce
- 2 tablespoons clear honey
- 25 g (1 oz) stem ginger, drained and finely chopped
- 2 spring onions, cut into long strips
- finely grated rind (zest) and juice of ½ lime
- black pepper
- lime wedges to serve

serves 4

1 Place the salmon fillets in a shallow non-metallic dish. Mix together the oil, soy sauce, honey, ginger, spring onions, lime rind and juice and seasoning. Pour over the fillets and turn to coat. Cover and marinate in the refrigerator for 30 minutes to 1 hour.

2 Preheat the grill to high. Lightly oil a baking tray. Lift the fillets and spring onions out of the marinade and place on the baking tray. Brush the fillets with a little of the marinade, then cook for 3 minutes. Turn over, brush with more of the marinade and grill for 3-5 minutes until cooked through. Garnish with lime wedges.

1

2

Nutritional value per serve Fat: 7.3 g Carbohydrate: 2.7 g Protein: 13.9 g

Coconut prawns and scallops

Preparation time 15 minutes, plus 30 minutes refrigeration Cooking time 15 minutes

Ingredients

1 kg (2 lb) large green prawns, shelled and deveined, tails left intact

3 egg whites, lightly beaten

90 g (3 oz) shredded coconut

vegetable oil for deep-frying

1 tablespoon peanut oil

4 fresh red chillies, deseeded and sliced

2 small fresh green chillies, deseeded and sliced

2 cloves garlic, crushed

1 tablespoon shredded fresh ginger

3 kaffir lime leaves, finely shredded

375 g (12 oz) scallops

125 g (4 oz) snow pea (mangetout) sprouts or leaves

2 tablespoons palm or brown sugar

4 tablespoons lime juice

2 tablespoons thai fish sauce

1 lime for garnish

serves 6

1 Dip prawns into the beaten egg white, then press into the shredded coconut to coat both sides. Place in single layer on a flat tray, cover and refrigerate 30 minutes.

2 Heat a large wok and add enough oil to be at least 5 cm (2-in.) deep. Add prawns, a few at a time and cook for 2–3 minutes or until golden and crisp. Drain on absorbent kitchen paper and keep warm. Drain oil from wok.

3 Reheat the wok over a high heat. Add peanut oil, chillies, garlic, ginger and lime leaves and stir-fry for 2–3 minutes or until fragrant. Add scallops to wok and stir-fry for 3 minutes or until opaque.

4 Add snow pea sprouts or leaves, sugar, lime juice and fish sauce and stir-fry for 2 minutes or until heated. Divide between serving bowls and top each with cooked prawns. Garnish with lime twists or quarters.

1

2

4

Nutritional value per serve Fat: 3.8 g Carbohydrate: 4.4 g Protein: 6.7 g

Char-grilled tuna with peach salsa

Preparation time 20 minutes, plus 1 hour refrigeration Cooking time 10 minutes

Ingredients

4 (about 180 g, 6 oz) tuna steaks
1 tablespoon olive oil
coriander chopped to garnish
lime wedges to serve

Salsa

3 ripe peaches, peeled, stoned and finely chopped
4 spring onions, finely chopped
1/2 yellow capsicum (pepper), finely chopped
juice of 1/2 lime
1 tablespoon chopped coriander
black pepper

serves 4

1 In a small bowl, place peaches, spring onions, capsicum, lime juice, coriander and black pepper and mix well. Cover and refrigerate for 1 hour.

2 Preheat the barbecue to high. Brush tuna steaks with oil and season with pepper. Place on barbecue and cook for 3–5 minutes on each side, until flesh flakes when tested with a fork. Garnish with coriander and serve with the lime wedges and peach salsa.

Nutritional value per serve Fat: 13.7 g Carbohydrate: 35 g Protein: 8.5 g

Spaghettini and scallops with breadcrumbs

Preparation time 10 minutes Cooking time 15 minutes

Ingredients

- 400 g (13 oz) dried spaghettini
- 12 fresh scallops with their corals
- ½ cup (125 ml, 4 fl oz) extra virgin olive oil
- 50 g (2 oz) fresh breadcrumbs
- 4 tablespoons chopped flat-leaf parsley
- 2 cloves garlic, crushed
- 1 teaspoon dried chillies, crushed
- ½ cup (125 ml, 4 fl oz) dry white wine

serves 4

1 Cook spaghettini in a large pan of boiling water, until al dente. Drain well and set aside.

2 Detach corals from scallops and set aside. Slice scallops into 3 or 4 pieces. Heat 2 tablespoons of oil in a frying pan, add breadcrumbs and fry, stirring, until golden. Remove from pan and set aside.

3 Heat remaining oil in the pan, add 2 tablespoons of parsley, garlic and chilli. Cook for 2 minutes.

4 Add scallops and cook for 30 seconds, until starting to turn opaque. Add wine and the corals, cook for a further 30 seconds, add spaghettini and toss for 1 minute. Sprinkle with breadcrumbs and remaining parsley.

Nutritional value per serve Fat: 5.4 g Carbohydrate: 5 g Protein: 7.8 g

Spinach, fish and ricotta cannelloni

Preparation time 20 minutes Cooking time 55 minutes

Ingredients

- 500 g (1 lb) cod or haddock fillet
- 250 g (8 oz) dried spinach lasagne
- salt and black pepper
- 3 tablespoons butter
- 1 small onion, chopped
- 3 tablespoons plain flour
- 2 cups (500 ml, 16 fl oz) milk
- 1 tablespoon snipped fresh chives
- juice of 1/2 lemon
- 30g (1 oz) frozen spinach, defrosted
- 250 g (8 oz) ricotta cheese
- 1 teaspoon chopped fresh parsley
- 1 teaspoon chopped fresh basil
- 425 g (14 oz) can chopped tomatoes
- 2 tablespoons fresh white breadcrumbs
- 2 tablespoons grated cheddar cheese

serves 4

1 Preheat oven to 180°C (350°F, gas mark 4). Place fish in a large saucepan, cover with cold water and simmer for 10 minutes until cooked through. Flake, discarding skin and bones, and set aside. Cook lasagne for 2 minutes in boiling water. Drain, rinse and pat dry with kitchen towels.

2 Heat 1 tablespoon of butter in a pan. Gently cook onion for 2–3 minutes, until golden. Add flour and cook, stirring, for 1 minute. Remove from heat and slowly stir in milk. Return to heat, bring to the boil, stirring until thickened. Add chives, lemon juice and seasoning.

3 Heat remaining butter in a large pan, add fish, ricotta and herbs. Mix to combine. Squeeze any moisture from spinach and fold into fish mixture. Combine to heat through. Spoon a little mixture onto each lasagne sheet and roll into tubes. Pour tomatoes into a 25 cm (10-in.) square ovenproof dish. Place tubes on top, pour over white sauce and sprinkle with breadcrumbs and cheddar. Cook in the oven for 30–35 minutes, until golden.

1

3

Nutritional value per serve Fat: 8.8 g Carbohydrate: 0.8 g Protein: 15.4 g

Chinese-style steamed grey mullet

Preparation time 10 minutes, plus 30 minutes refrigeration Cooking time 20 minutes

Ingredients

1 grey mullet, about 700 g (1 lb 7 oz), scaled and gutted

½ teaspoon salt

1 tablespoon vegetable oil

1 tablespoon light soy sauce

1 large carrot, cut into fine strips

4 spring onions, cut into fine strips

1 tablespoon grated fresh root ginger

1 tablespoon sesame oil (optional)

fresh coriander to garnish

serves 2

1 In a small bowl, combine salt, vegetable oil and soy sauce. Make 4 deep slashes along each side of the fish, and rub inside and out with the sauce mixture. Cover and place in the refrigerator for 30 minutes.

2 Spread half the carrot, spring onions and ginger in the centre of a large piece of foil. Place the fish on top, then sprinkle with the remaining vegetables and ginger and any remaining oil mixture.

3 Loosely fold over the foil and seal. Transfer the fish to a steamer or a rack set over a roasting tin half filled with water. Cover the steamer tightly with a lid or the roasting pan with foil. Cook for 20 minutes or until the fish is firm and cooked through. Put the sesame oil, if using, into a small saucepan and heat. Drizzle over the fish and garnish with coriander.

2

3

Nutritional value per serve Fat: 4.8 g Carbohydrate: 0.9 g Protein: 19.4 g

Home-smoked trout

Preparation time 15 minutes, plus 1 hour standing Cooking time 20 minutes

Ingredients

- 125 g (4 oz) smoking chips
- 1/2 cup (125 ml, 4 fl oz) white wine
- 4 small rainbow trout, cleaned, with head and tail intact
- 1 tablespoon vegetable oil
- 3 red onions, thinly sliced
- 1 lemon, thinly sliced
- 8 sprigs dill

serves 4

1 Place smoking chips and wine in a large glass dish and stand for 1 hour.

2 Preheat covered barbecue to a low heat. Place smoking chips dish in barbecue over hot coals, cover barbecue with lid and heat for 5–10 minutes or until liquid is hot.

3 Place trout on a wire rack set in a roasting tin. Brush trout lightly with oil, then top with onions, lemon and dill. Place on rack in barbecue, cover and smoke for 15–20 minutes or until trout flakes when tested with fork.

1

2

3

Nutritional value per serve Fat: 5.4 g Carbohydrate: 2.1 g Protein: 6.7 g

Couscous salad with seafood and fresh mint

Preparation time 20 minutes Cooking time 5 minutes

Ingredients

- ½ cup (125 ml, 4 fl oz) olive oil
- 2 tablespoons lemon juice
- 1 large clove garlic, finely chopped
- 1 teaspoon celery seed
- ¼ teaspoon turmeric
- ¼ teaspoon cumin
- 1⅔ cups (410 ml, 13 fl oz) vegetable stock
- 500 g (1 lb) raw king prawns, peeled (tails on)
- 200 g (7 oz) small calamari (squid) rings
- 300 g (10 oz) couscous
- 3 tomatoes, finely diced
- 2 stalks celery, finely sliced
- 6 spring onions, chopped
- 20 fresh mint leaves, finely sliced
- salt and pepper

serves 6

1 Whisk together oil, lemon juice, garlic and celery seed until thick. Season with salt and pepper. In a pan, bring stock to the boil and add turmeric and cumin. Add prawns and calamari. Poach gently for 2 minutes until the prawns are orange. Remove seafood from stock with a slotted spoon.

2 In a large bowl, place the couscous and pour over hot stock. Stir well and cover. Allow to stand for about 10 minutes until water is absorbed.

3 Toss couscous with a fork to fluff then add seafood. Toss in the diced tomatoes, celery, spring onions and some of the shredded mint leaves.

4 Add the dressing and mix well then garnish with remaining mint leaves.

Those who enjoy meat will love these succulent beef, lamb and pork recipes. Discover curries, meatballs, stir-fries, roasts, grills, casseroles, ribs and skewers, as well as ideas for incorporating meat in soups and salads.

Many cuts and types of meat are teamed here with vegetables, ingredients and accompaniments, such as spices, marinades, salsas, sauces, that really bring something new to the table. You'll find some more great recipes featuring meat in the section Rice, Pasta and Noodles.

Meat is a supplier of high quality protein, containing the eight essential amino acids required by the body, and of iron. The iron in meat is readily absorbed and used by the body. With all the B group vitamins and zinc present, lean beef, veal, trim lamb and pork are a unique combination of many essential nutrients.

Tips on cooking meat

Grilling and pan-frying

- Trim the fat from the edge of steak and chops. To prevent the meat curling up while cooking, make a few small cuts around the edge, just past the gristle line into the meat.
- Season grilled and pan-fried meats with pepper and herbs before cooking, but sprinkle with salt during or after cooking.
- Oil sprays are a convenient and low-fat way of lubricating the pan and the meat before cooking.
- When grilling or barbecuing meat, do not turn it often. Cook the first side for 1–2 minutes to seal, turn the meat over and cook the second side for 3–4 minutes to complete cooking.

Casseroles, stewing and braising

When browning meat cubes, heat just enough oil to coat the bottom of the pan. Meat will not brown in a lot of oil. Do not overcrowd the pan. Brown the meat in batches of 250 g (8 oz) each.

When stewing or braising meat, use a saucepan large enough to amply accommodate the food. The food should only half fill the saucepan to allow the rising steam and condensation cycle to assist the cooking process. Cover it with a tight-fitting lid.

Oven roasting

- Trim the thickest parts of fat from the meat.
- Place the meat either on a rack in a baking dish or straight in a dish. Add a cup of water to protect the meat juices from charring. If the liquid dries out, add a little more.
- When the roast is cooked, move it to a plate, cover it and let it rest for 10 minutes before carving.

Nutritional value per serve Fat: 3.2 g Carbohydrate: 5.2 g Protein: 3.6 g

Middle eastern spinach and meatball soup

Preparation time 15 minutes Cooking time 1 hour

Ingredients
2 tablespoons olive oil
2 large leeks, washed and sliced
1 tablespoon turmeric
1 tablespoon cinnamon
125 g (4 oz) yellow split peas
1½ litres (3 pints) vegetable stock or water
500 g (1 lb) spinach, washed and chopped
400 g (13 oz) potatoes, peeled and diced
4 tablespoons rice flour
juice of 2 lemons
salt and ground pepper
3 tablespoons yoghurt
oil for frying
4 golden shallots, thinly sliced
10 mint leaves, finely sliced
Meatballs
1 large brown onion, finely minced
250 g (8 oz) minced lamb
2 cloves garlic, minced
salt and pepper
serves 4

1 Heat the olive oil in a large saucepan. Add the sliced leeks and sauté until golden. Add the turmeric and cinnamon and stir over heat for 1 minute. Add the split peas and stock or water and bring to the boil. Reduce heat and simmer for 30 minutes.

2 In a large bowl, mix together the onion, lamb, garlic and salt and pepper to taste. Shape the meat mixture into walnut-sized balls. Drop them into the soup and simmer for 10 minutes. Add the spinach and potato and continue simmering a further 10 minutes.

3 Mix the rice flour with a little water and lemon juice until smooth. Stir into the soup. Add salt and pepper to taste and simmer for 10 minutes. Reduce heat and stir yoghurt through. Heat on low for 1 minute without boiling.

4 In a separate frying pan, heat the oil and fry the shallots until crisp and golden. To serve, garnish the soup with the fried shallots and mint leaves.

Nutritional value per serve Fat: 6.3 g Carbohydrate: 4.8 g Protein: 10.5 g

Pork in walnut sauce

Preparation time 10 minutes, plus 1 hour resting Cooking time 1¾ hours

Ingredients

- 1½ kg (3 lb) lean pork, loin or leg
- coarse salt
- 1 tablespoon soft butter
- freshly grated nutmeg
- freshly ground black pepper
- 1 tablespoon brandy
- 1 litre (1⅔ pints) milk
- 150 g (5 oz) shelled walnuts, scalded and peeled if desired
- 2 large red apples, sliced into rounds
- extra 2 teaspoons soft butter
- 2 teaspoons lemon juice
- pinch of cinnamon
- mashed potato to serve

serves 6

1 Sprinkle the pork with salt and leave for about 1 hour. Preheat the oven to 200°C (400°F, gas mark 6).

2 Rub the meat with 1 tablespoon butter, and season with nutmeg and pepper. Heat a large, heavy-based pan. Add pork and brown on all sides. Pour over the brandy and flame.

3 Place the meat in a fairly deep dish that will hold the meat snugly. Cover with milk and put in the oven on a low rack (or upturned plate). Cook for about 1½ hours. After about an hour add the walnuts. Adjust the seasoning and add more milk if necessary.

4 Place apple slices on a buttered flat oven tray and sprinkle tops with lemon juice and cinnamon. Place in the oven for 10 minutes or until soft and a rosy colour. Remove the cooked meat from the oven and stand for 10 minutes. Slice the meat, and serve the sauce separately. Accompany with the mashed potato and apple slices.

2

3

Nutritional value per serve Fat: 7.7 g Carbohydrate: 2.2 g Protein: 21.4 g

Lemongrass pork skewers

Preparation time 15 minutes, plus 20 minutes marinating

Cooking time 3 minutes approximately

Ingredients
500 g (1 lb) piece pork leg steak, or scotch fillet
32 short bamboo skewers, soaked
oil for greasing
sweet chilli sauce for serving
Marinade
3 garlic cloves, crushed
2 tablespoons chopped fresh lemongrass
2 tablespoons finely chopped coriander stalks
1 tablespoon brown sugar
1/2 teaspoon ground coriander
1/4 teaspoon white pepper
2 tablespoons soy sauce
2 tablespoons fish sauce
2 tablespoons sesame oil
75 ml (2 1/2 fl oz) cold water

makes 32

1 Cut pork across the grain into thin strips. Thread 1–2 strips onto each skewer and place into a glass container. In a bowl, mix together the garlic, lemongrass, coriander stalks, sugar, ground coriander, pepper, soy sauce, fish sauce, sesame oil and water. Pour over the skewers and marinate for 20 minutes or longer.

2 Heat a nonstick pan, barbecue plate or grill. Brush with oil and place on the skewers. Cook for 1–2 minutes each side, brushing with marinade as they cook. Serve with sweet chilli sauce.

1

2

Nutritional value per serve Fat: 7.4 g Carbohydrate: 14 g Protein: 7.4 g

Gnocchi with pork and capsicums

Preparation time 20 minutes, plus 1 hour marinating Cooking time 35 minutes

Ingredients
360 g (12 oz) pork steak, cubed
4 cloves garlic, crushed
1 tablespoon dried oregano
juice of 1/2 lemon
1/2 cup (125 ml, 4 fl oz) extra virgin olive oil
salt and black pepper
1 small onion, finely chopped
1/2 stick celery, finely chopped
3 tablespoons finely chopped fresh parsley
250 g (8 oz) yellow capsicums (peppers), chopped
220 ml (7 1/2 fl oz) tomato paste
3 tablespoons beef stock
800 g (1lb 10 oz) fresh gnocchi
25 g (1 oz) pitted black olives, sliced
serves 4

1 Place pork in a shallow, non-metallic dish. Mix in half the garlic, oregano, lemon juice, 1 tablespoon of oil and seasoning. Cover and refrigerate for 1 hour.

2 Heat remaining oil in a large pan. Add onion and a pinch of salt. Cook for 5 minutes until softened. Stir in remaining garlic, celery, parsley and peppers, and cook over a low heat for 10 minutes.

3 Stir in the tomato paste and simmer for a further 10 minutes, stirring often. Add pork, marinade and stock. Simmer, uncovered, for 10 minutes or until thickened and cooked through, stirring occasionally.

4 Cook gnocchi in a large pan of boiling water, until al dente. Drain and transfer to a large serving bowl. Spoon over the sauce and toss to combine. Sprinkle with olives.

Nutritional value per serve Fat: 4.1 g Carbohydrate: 5.4 g Protein: 7.8 g

Pan-fried pork steaks with orange and sage

Preparation time 10 minutes Cooking time 20 minutes

Ingredients
1 tablespoon olive oil
salt and black pepper
12 thin-cut pork loin steaks
300 ml (10 fl oz) chicken stock
freshly grated rind (zest) and juice of 1 orange
2 tablespoons dry sherry or vermouth
2 tablespoons redcurrant jelly
2 teaspoons chopped fresh sage
lettuce to serve
serves 4–6

1 Heat the oil in a large, heavy-based frying pan. Season the steaks with salt and pepper. Add 6 steaks to the pan and fry for 2–3 minutes on each side or until cooked. Remove to a heated plate, cover and keep warm. Cook remaining steaks and remove to the plate.

2 Add the stock, orange rind and juice, sherry or vermouth and redcurrant jelly to the pan. Cook vigorously over a high heat, stirring until reduced by half.

3 Stir the sage into the sauce and season to taste. Return the steaks to the pan and heat for 1–2 minutes to warm through, spooning the sauce over to glaze. Serve 2–3 steaks on a bed of shredded lettuce and drizzle over the sauce.

Nutritional value per serve Fat: 15.8 g Carbohydrate: 3.4 g Protein: 24.5 g

Glazed pork spare ribs

Preparation time 10 minutes, plus 30 minutes marinating Cooking time 1 hour 10 minutes

Ingredients

- 1 tablespoon soy sauce
- 2 tablespoons white-wine vinegar
- 3 tablespoons hoisin or oyster sauce
- 2 tablespoons honey
- 2 cloves garlic, crushed
- 2½ cm (1-in.) piece fresh ginger root, peeled and grated
- 2 teaspoons vegetable oil
- ½ teaspoon five-spice powder
- 1 tablespoon brown sugar
- 1½–2 kg (3–4 lb) American style pork spare ribs

serves 6

1 In a saucepan, combine soy sauce, white-wine vinegar, hoisin or oyster sauce, honey, garlic, ginger, oil, five-spice powder and sugar. Stir well and bring to the boil. Remove from heat. Place pork in a large pie dish. Spread half of the marinade over the ribs to cover all surfaces. Cover and stand 30 minutes.

2 Preheat the oven to 220°C (425°F, gas mark 7). Place the ribs on a rack in a baking dish and pour some water under the rack to prevent drippings from charring. Bake for 30 minutes. Reduce heat to 180°C (350°F, gas mark 4) and bake for 40 minutes, brushing well with remaining marinade every 15 minutes to glaze. Serve immediately.

1

2

Nutritional value per serve Fat: 9.1 g Carbohydrate: 0.4 g Protein: 25.9 g

Herbed and spiced pork loin

Preparation time 30 minutes, plus overnight marinating

Cooking time 2½ hours, plus 15 minutes standing

Ingredients
2 kg (4 lb) boneless pork loin, rolled and rind scored at 1 cm (½-in.) intervals
Herb and spice marinade
1 onion, chopped
2 tablespoons pink peppercorns, crushed
2 tablespoons crushed green peppercorns
2 tablespoons ground coriander
1 tablespoon freshly ground black pepper
1 tablespoon ground cumin
1 teaspoon garam masala
1 teaspoon ground mixed spice
1 teaspoon turmeric
1 teaspoon paprika
1 teaspoon sea salt
2 tablespoons peanut oil
2 tablespoons sesame oil
1 tablespoon white vinegar
serves 8

1 In a food processor or blender, place onion, peppercorns, coriander, black pepper, cumin, garam masala, mixed spice, turmeric, paprika, salt, peanut oil, sesame oil and vinegar and process to a smooth paste.

2 Rub marinade over pork, place in a large glass dish, cover and refrigerate overnight.

3 Place pork on a wire rack set in a baking dish and bake at 190°C (375°F, gas mark 5) for 1 hour.

4 Preheat barbecue to a medium heat. Transfer pork to lightly oiled barbecue grill and cook, turning frequently, for 1½ hours or until tender and cooked through. Stand for 15 minutes before carving and serving.

Nutritional value per serve Fat: 8.5 g Carbohydrate: 1.9 g Protein: 14.7 g

Thai beef salad with chilli lime dressing

Preparation time 20 minutes Cooking time 25 minutes, plus 20 minutes resting

Ingredients
500 g (1 lb) beef tenderloin (fillet) in one piece
2 cloves garlic, crushed
3 tablespoons chopped fresh coriander
2 tablespoons olive oil
1 tablespoon sweet chilli sauce
2 tablespoons lime juice
2 teaspoons thai fish sauce
2 teaspoons soft light brown sugar
1/2 teaspoon ground cumin
250 g (8 oz) mixed salad leaves, washed and crisped
3 tablespoons fresh mint leaves
3 spring onions, diagonally sliced
1 red capsicum (pepper), sliced for garnish
serves 4

1 Preheat oven to 220°C (425°F, gas mark 7). Trim off the silvery membrane and brush the fillet with oil. Place in a shallow tray and roast in oven for 25 minutes until medium rare. If using a meat thermometer, cook until it reaches 65°C to 70°C (135°F).

2 Remove from oven, cover with foil and rest for 20 minutes. Hold the end firmly with a strip of foil and using a sharp knife, slice very finely.

3 In a bowl, combine garlic, coriander, oil, chilli sauce, lime juice, fish sauce, sugar and cumin. Arrange salad leaves on a serving platter, drizzle with some of the dressing. Arrange the beef slices on top and pour over remaining dressing. Sprinkle with mint leaves, spring onions and capsicum strips.

Nutritional value per serve Fat: 3 g Carbohydrate: 2.1 g Protein: 9.4 g

Keema curry

Preparation time 10 minutes Cooking time 40–45 minutes

Ingredients
1 tablespoon vegetable oil
1 onion, finely chopped
2½ cm (1-in.) piece fresh root ginger, grated
2 cloves garlic, crushed
500 g (1 lb) lean minced lamb
2 teaspoons ground turmeric
1 teaspoon chilli powder
1 tablespoon garam masala
3 tablespoons tomato paste
450 ml (14 fl oz) lamb stock
125 g (4 oz) frozen peas
salt and black pepper
2 tablespoons chopped fresh coriander
extra coriander to garnish
serves 4

1 Heat the oil in a wok or large, heavy-based frying pan. Add the onion, ginger and garlic and cook over a low heat for 5 minutes or until softened. Add minced lamb, stir to break up with the back of a wooden spoon. Cook while stirring for 10 minutes or until the lamb browns.

2 Pour off any excess fat from the pan. Add the turmeric, chilli, garam masala and tomato paste, and stir-fry for 1–2 minutes. Add the stock and bring to the boil, stirring. Reduce the heat, cover and simmer for 15 minutes.

3 Add the peas and simmer for 10 minutes longer. Remove from the heat, stir in the salt, pepper and coriander. Garnish with coriander.

1

2

Nutritional value per serve Fat: 4 g Carbohydrate: 9.6 g Protein: 8.8 g

Honey beef with pineapple salsa

Preparation time 8 minutes Cooking time 8 minutes

Ingredients

1 tablespoon vegetable oil
2 tablespoons sesame seeds
2 cloves garlic, crushed
500 g (1 lb) lean beef strips
185 g (6 oz) snow peas (mangetout), trimmed
2 zucchini (courgettes), chopped
3 tablespoons honey
2 tablespoons soy sauce
1 tablespoon oyster sauce
steamed rice to serve

Pineapple salsa

½ fresh pineapple, peeled, cored and diced
1 fresh red chilli, chopped
2 tablespoons brown sugar
2 tablespoons snipped fresh chives
2 tablespoons lime juice

serves 4

1 In a bowl, place the pineapple, chilli, sugar, chives and lime juice and toss to combine. Set aside.

2 Heat 2 teaspoons oil in a wok over a medium heat. Add sesame seeds and garlic and stir-fry for 2 minutes or until seeds are golden. Remove seed mixture from wok with a slotted spoon and set aside.

3 Add remaining oil to wok. Add half the beef and stir-fry for 2 minutes or until brown, remove. Stir-fry the remaining beef adding extra oil if needed.

4 Add snow peas, zucchini, combined honey, soy and oyster sauces and sesame seed mixture. Stir-fry for 3 minutes or until sauce thickens. Remove to a platter. Serve immediately with pineapple salsa and steamed rice.

2

3

4

Nutritional value per serve Fat: 8.1 g Carbohydrate: 5.3 g Protein: 15.8 g

Korean marinated beef strips

Preparation time 20 minutes, plus 4 hours marinating Cooking time 10 minutes

Ingredients

- 500 g (1 lb) lean beef fillet, sliced into 5 mm (1/4-in.) thick strips
- 2 spring onions, chopped
- vegetable oil for brushing
- chilli sauce to serve
- extra spring onions to garnish

Marinade

- 2 tablespoons sesame seeds
- 2 cloves garlic, finely chopped
- 2 1/2 cm (3/4-in) piece fresh root ginger, finely chopped
- 2 tablespoons sugar
- 3 tablespoons light soy sauce
- 3 tablespoons dark soy sauce
- 1 tablespoon sesame oil

serves 4

1 Heat a frying pan. Add the sesame seeds and dry-fry until golden, stirring constantly. Place in a small food processor or blender and grind finely. Add the garlic, ginger, sugar, light and dark soy sauces and oil and process or blend to a paste. In a non-metallic bowl, mix together the beef, spring onions and spice paste, turning to coat. Cover and marinate in the refrigerator for 4 hours.

2 Brush a ridged, cast-iron grill pan or large, heavy-based frying pan with the oil and heat until very hot. Add the beef strips in a single layer (in batches if necessary) and cook for 1–2 minutes, turning once, until browned. Serve with chilli sauce, garnished with spring onions.

Nutritional value per serve Fat: 3.4 g Carbohydrate: 3.7 g Protein: 7.5 g

Steak au poivre

Preparation time 8 minutes Cooking time 10 minutes

Ingredients

3 tablespoons mixed peppercorns
4 thick beef fillet steaks (about 160 g, 5 oz each)
2 tablespoons olive oil
400 ml (13 fl oz) red wine
100 ml ($3^1/_2$ fl oz) water
salt
french fries or new potatoes to serve
salad to serve

serves 4

1 Crush the peppercorns with a pestle and mortar or the end of a rolling pin. Brush the steaks with 1 tablespoon of the oil. Press the peppercorns around the edge of each steak with your fingers.

2 Heat the remaining oil in a large, heavy-based frying pan over a medium to high heat. Add the steaks and cook for 5–6 minutes according to thickness, turning once, until cooked to your liking.

3 Transfer the steaks to serving plates and keep warm. Lower the heat and pour in the wine and water. Bring to the boil and cook for 4 minutes or until reduced by half, stirring constantly. Add salt to taste and spoon the sauce over the steaks to serve. Serve with french fries or new potatoes and a leafy salad.

Nutritional value per serve Fat: 8.4 g Carbohydrate: 10.5 g Protein: 11.3 g

Indonesian beef curry

Preparation time 8 minutes Cooking time 3 hours, 15 minutes

Ingredients
2 stalks lemongrass, peeled and chopped
4 tablespoons desiccated coconut, toasted
2 onions, chopped
2 cloves garlic, chopped
5 cm (2-in.) piece fresh root ginger, chopped
1 red chilli, deseeded and chopped
2 tablespoons vegetable oil
750 g (1½ lb) topside beef, cut into 2½ cm (¾-in.) cubes
1 teaspoon turmeric
400 ml (13 fl oz) can coconut milk
1 teaspoon sugar
salt
extra red chilli, deseeded and sliced for garnish
rice to serve
serves 4

1 Peel the outer layers from the lemongrass stalks, then finely chop the lower white bulbous part. In a food processor, finely grind the toasted coconut and set aside. Process the lemongrass, onions, garlic, ginger and chilli to a paste.

2 Heat the oil in a frying pan and fry the paste for 5 minutes to release the flavours, stirring often. Add the beef, stir to coat and fry for 3–4 minutes, until sealed.

3 Add the ground coconut, turmeric, coconut milk, sugar and salt and mix well. Bring to the boil while stirring, then reduce the heat. Simmer, covered, for 3 hours, stirring from time to time, until the sauce reduces to a rich gravy. Garnish with the sliced chilli. Serve with rice.

Nutritional value per serve Fat: 4.7 g Carbohydrate: 11 g Protein: 6.5 g

Indian meatballs in tomato sauce

Preparation time 20 minutes Cooking time 45 minutes

Ingredients

- 500 g (1 lb) minced lamb
- 5 tablespoons natural yoghurt
- 5 cm (2-in.) piece fresh root ginger, finely chopped
- 1 green chilli, deseeded and finely chopped
- 3 tablespoons chopped fresh coriander
- 2 teaspoons ground cumin
- 2 teaspoons ground coriander
- salt and black pepper
- 2 tablespoons vegetable oil
- 1 onion, chopped
- 2 cloves garlic, chopped
- ½ teaspoon turmeric
- 1 teaspoon garam masala
- 400 g (13 oz) can chopped tomatoes
- 150 ml (5 fl oz) water
- rice to serve

serves 4

1 In a large bowl, mix together the lamb, 1 tablespoon yoghurt, ginger, chilli, 2 tablespoons coriander, cumin, ground coriander, salt and pepper. With wet hands, shape the mixture into 16 balls.

2 Heat 1 tablespoon of oil in a large saucepan. Add half the meatballs and cook until brown well all over. Remove, drain on kitchen paper and set aside. Repeat with remaining meatballs.

3 Heat the remaining oil in the pan. Add the onion and garlic and fry for 5 minutes or until softened, stirring occasionally. Stir in the turmeric, garam masala and remaining yoghurt, 1 tablespoon at a time.

4 Add the tomatoes and their juice, meatballs and water and bring to the boil. Partly cover the pan, reduce the heat and simmer for 30 minutes, stirring occasionally. Sprinkle over the rest of the coriander to garnish. Serve with rice.

Nutritional value per serve Fat: 12.5 g Carbohydrate: 2 g Protein: 13.6 g

Warm steak salad with pawpaw and spanish onion

Preparation time 20 minutes, plus 35 minutes refrigeration Cooking time 4 minutes

Ingredients

- 750 g (1½ lb) beef tenderloin (fillet steak), trimmed
- 1 tablespoon finely chopped rosemary
- ¼ teaspoon cayenne pepper
- 1 tablespoon butter
- 2 teaspoons oil
- 1 small pawpaw (papaya), peeled, deseeded and cut into bite-size cubes
- 1 small spanish onion, thinly sliced
- 1 small bunch endive (curly chicory), torn into bite-size pieces
- 2 oranges, segmented

Dressing

- 2 tablespoons red-wine vinegar
- 5 tablespoons olive oil
- salt and freshly ground black pepper

serves 4–6

1 Whisk together vinegar, 5 tablespoons of oil, salt and pepper and set aside. Trim silver membrane from beef tenderloin. With a sharp knife thinly slice, then cut each slice into strips. To make slicing easier, place the meat in the freezer for 35 minutes until it begins to firm up.

2 Sprinkle meat strips with rosemary and cayenne. Heat the butter and oil in a large, heavy-based frying pan, add half of the meat and cook over high heat for 1–2 minutes, tossing gently. Remove to a bowl and cook remainder.

3 Mix the pawpaw and spanish onion into the steak strips. Add dressing and toss well.

4 Combine together endive and orange segments. Place on a serving platter and pile the beef strips in the centre. Serve immediately.

2

3

4

Nutritional value per serve Fat: 5.4 g Carbohydrate: 19 g Protein: 12.6 g

Lamb fillets with salsa pilaf

Preparation time 10 minutes, plus 30 minutes standing Cooking time 25 minutes

Ingredients

- 750 g (1½ lb) lamb fillets
- ½ teaspoon crushed garlic
- 1 tablespoon lemon juice
- 2 teaspoons olive oil
- salt and pepper
- 1¼ cups (250 g, 8 oz) long-grain rice
- 1½ litres (2½ pints) boiling water
- 60 g (2 oz) pine nuts, toasted
- 300 g (10 oz) jar tomato salsa
- 2 tablespoons currants

serves 4–5

1 Trim the lamb fillets, removing the fine silver membrane. Place in a dish and add garlic, lemon juice, oil, salt and pepper. Cover and stand for 30 minutes. Cook the rice in salted boiling water for about 15 minutes, until tender. Drain well and keep hot.

2 Heat a small frying pan, add pine nuts and shake over heat until coloured. Add the salsa and currants and heat through.

3 Heat grill plate and oil lightly, set at medium-high. Place lamb on grill and cook 6–8 minutes, turning to cook on all sides. Cook longer for well done. Rest 5 minutes before slicing into 1 cm (½-in.) diagonal cut slices.

4 Using a cup or mould, form a mound of rice on the plate. Pour salsa over the rice and arrange lamb slices at base.

Nutritional value per serve Fat: 11.3 g Carbohydrate: 22 g Protein: 9.9 g

Macaroni with lamb ragoût

Preparation time 15 minutes Cooking time 20 minutes

Ingredients
2 tablespoons olive oil
4 tablespoons butter
1 stick celery, finely chopped
1 onion, finely chopped
1 small carrot, finely chopped
360 g (12 oz) minced lamb
black pepper
1 cup (250 ml, 8 fl oz) milk
400 g (13 oz) dried macaroni
2 tablespoons chopped fresh mint
parmesan cheese, grated
serves 4

1 Heat oil and butter in a large frying pan. Gently fry celery, onion and carrot for 5–7 minutes, until softened. Add lamb and cook, stirring, for 5–6 minutes, until meat has browned. Season.

2 Reduce heat to very low, stir in milk a little at a time, until milk is absorbed with each addition, and mixture is cooked through.

3 Cook pasta in a large pan of boiling water, until al dente. Drain. Garnish with mint and sprinkle with extra parmesan.

Nutritional value per serve Fat: 4.5 g Carbohydrate: 5.9 g Protein: 7 g

Lamb shanks with broad beans, olives and risoni

Preparation time 10 minutes Cooking time 1 hour

Ingredients

- 2 tablespoons olive oil
- 2 cloves garlic, crushed
- 4 lamb shanks
- 1 onion, chopped
- 2 cups (500 ml, 16 fl oz) beef stock
- 4 sprigs oregano
- 2 tablespoons tomato paste
- 2 cups (500 ml, 16 fl oz) water
- 100 g (3½ oz) risoni pasta
- 125 g (4 oz) frozen broad beans, thawed
- 160 g (5½ oz) black olives
- 2 teaspoons chopped fresh oregano
- salt and freshly ground pepper

serves 4–6

1 Heat oil in a large saucepan. Add garlic, lamb shanks and onion, and cook for 5 minutes until shanks are lightly browned. Add the beef stock, oregano, tomato paste and half the water. Bring to the boil, reduce heat, and cover and simmer for 45 minutes. Remove shanks, slice meat off bone, and set aside.

2 Add the risoni and remaining water, and cook for a further 5 minutes. Add broad beans, olives, meat, oregano, salt and pepper. Cook for 5 minutes, and serve.

Nutritional value per serve Fat: 6.4 g Carbohydrate: 0.5 g Protein: 14.6 g

Lamb with lemon and garlic

Preparation time 8 minutes Cooking time 60–70 minutes

Ingredients

3 tablespoons olive oil
1 kg (2 lb) lean, boneless lamb, cut into 2½ cm (¾-in.) pieces
1 spanish onion, finely chopped
3 cloves garlic, crushed
1 tablespoon paprika
3 tablespoons finely chopped fresh parsley
3 tablespoons fresh lemon juice
½ cup (125 ml, 4 fl oz) stock or water
salt and pepper
3 tablespoons dry white wine (optional)

serves 3–6

1 In a large, heavy-based pan, heat oil. Add half of the lamb and brown well on all sides. Remove to a plate and repeat with remaining lamb. Remove and cover to keep warm.

2 Stir onion into pan and cook about 5 minutes, until softened. Stir in garlic and cook 2 minutes, then stir in paprika. Return the lamb to the pan with any juices on plate. Add the parsley, lemon juice, stock or water, salt and pepper. Cover tightly and cook over very low heat for 50–60 minutes, shaking pan occasionally, until lamb is very tender. If necessary, add wine or 3 tablespoons water.

Nutritional value per serve Fat: 5.5 g Carbohydrate: 1.5 g Protein: 16.8 g

Greek shish kebabs

Preparation time 20 minutes, plus 4 hours marinating or overnight
Cooking time 10–12 minutes

Ingredients
750 g (1½ lb) lamb neck fillet, cut into 2½ cm (¾-in.) pieces
fresh mint to garnish
lemon wedges to serve
Marinade
100 g (3½ oz) greek yoghurt
½ onion, grated
2 cloves garlic, crushed
juice of ½ lemon
1 tablespoon olive oil
3 tablespoons chopped fresh mint
salt and black pepper
8 small metal skewers
makes 8

1 Preheat barbecue to a high heat.

2 In a large bowl, combine yoghurt, onion, garlic, lemon juice, oil, mint and seasoning. Add lamb and toss to coat. Cover and refrigerate for 4 hours or overnight.

3 Thread lamb onto metal skewers. Cook kebabs on barbecue for 10–12 minutes, turning 2–3 times, until cooked through. Garnish with mint and serve with lemon wedges.

Nutritional value per serve Fat: 8.5 g Carbohydrate: 4.7 g Protein: 11.9 g

Lamb with honeyed onions

Preparation time 20 minutes, plus 3 hours marinating Cooking time 20 minutes

Ingredients

12 lamb cutlets, trimmed of fat

Yoghurt marinade

1 tablespoon chopped fresh mint

1 clove garlic, crushed

200 g (7 oz) natural yoghurt

2 tablespoons wholegrain mustard

1 tablespoon mint sauce

Honeyed onions

2 tablespoons olive oil

2 red onions, sliced

1 tablespoon honey

2 tablespoons red-wine vinegar

serves 4–6

1 To make marinade: place mint, garlic, yoghurt, mustard and mint sauce in a large glass bowl and mix to combine. Add lamb, turn to coat, cover and refrigerate for 3 hours.

2 Preheat barbecue to a medium heat. For honeyed onions: heat oil on barbecue plate, add onions and cook, stirring constantly, for 10 minutes. Add honey and vinegar and cook, stirring, for a further 5 minutes or until onions are soft and golden.

3 Drain lamb, place on lightly oiled barbecue and cook for 2–3 minutes each side. Serve topped with onions.

1

2

Nutritional value per serve Fat: 22.7 g Carbohydrate: 12.7 g Protein: 12.7 g

Veal and peach melts

Preparation time 10 minutes Cooking time 6–8 minutes

Ingredients

- 1 tablespoon butter
- 1 tablespoon oil
- 4 large, thinly-sliced veal steaks
- salt and freshly ground black pepper
- 3 spring onions, finely chopped
- 200 g (7 oz) packet dried peaches
- 4 ready-sliced slices swiss cheese

serves 4

1 Heat a large, heavy-based frying pan, add half the butter and oil and swirl to cover the base. Add 2 steaks and cook very quickly on each side. Sprinkle steaks with salt and pepper as they cook. Remove to a plate and keep hot. Repeat with remaining steaks, adding remaining butter and oil if needed.

2 Reduce heat, add spring onions and sauté. Add peaches and sauté a little on each side.

3 Preheat oven to 180°C (350°F, gas mark 4). Cut steaks in half. Place half of each steak on oven tray and stack with peaches, spring onions, other half steak, peaches and top with a swiss cheese slice.

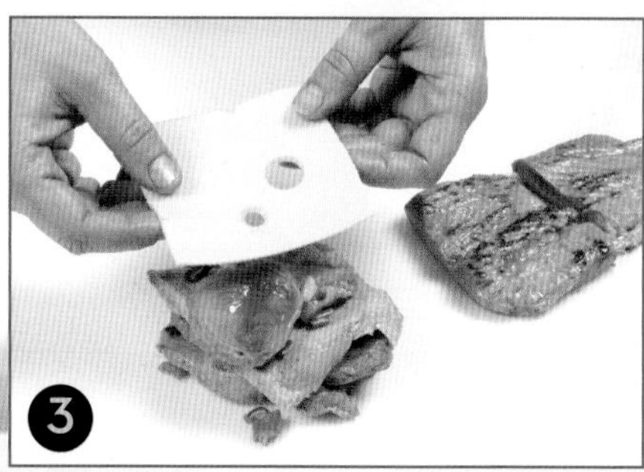

4 Place tray in preheated oven about 1½ minutes until cheese melts and encases the stack, or place under a hot griller. Serve immediately with vegetables.

There's lots of intriguing possibilities here to end a meal with, contribute to a morning or afternoon tea, make a supper or snack or go into a lunchbox. Some of these recipes can be produced in multiple servings or pieces for a party or a special occasion.

Fruit plays a large part in many of the dessert recipes, and chocolate has its place too. You'll find so many sweet recipes, you won't know which one to choose!

Tips on making muffins

Below are some useful tips for good results when making muffins:

- Preheat your oven. Muffins are usually cooked at a slightly higher temperature than cakes: as a rough guide at 200°C (400°F, gas mark 6).
- Don't worry if you don't have the exact muffin tin size – this usually just means you will end up with more or fewer muffins.
- Non-stick muffin pans come in a variety of sizes: 1 cup tin with 6 holes, a half-cup tin with 12 holes; a one-third-cup tin with 12 holes and mini-muffin tins with 12 holes. If you plan to line the holes with paper cases, do so before preparing the mixture. If the cases are thin, use a double layer to keep them in place.
- Sift the flour and dry ingredients into a large bowl. Make a well in the centre and set the bowl aside. Whisk the wet mixture thoroughly in a jug to make pouring easier.
- Do not over-mix the dry and liquid muffin ingredients – it should still be quite lumpy. Fill the tin holes only three-quarters full.
- You may need to turn the tin during cooking if the back of your oven is hotter than the front. A muffin is cooked if it comes away from the side of the tin. Otherwise, insert a skewer into the centre of the muffin; if it comes out clean, the muffin is cooked.

Nutritional value per serve Fat: 7 g Carbohydrate: 21.7 g Protein: 2.6 g

Fruit tartlets

Preparation time 30 minutes, plus 20 minutes refrigeration Cooking time 10–20 minutes

Ingredients

Pastry

- 185 g (6 oz) plain flour
- 2 tablespoons icing sugar
- 125 g (4 oz) butter
- 2 egg yolks
- 1 teaspoon water

Custard cream filling

- 125 g (4 oz) sugar
- 6 teaspoons cornflour
- 2 eggs
- 1 egg yolk
- 3/4 cup (185 ml, 6 fl oz) milk
- 4 tablespoons thickened cream
- 1 tablespoon orange-flavoured liqueur

Tartlet filling

- 1 teaspoon gelatine
- 90 ml (3 fl oz) boiling water
- 155 g (5 oz) apricot jam, warmed and sieved
- 2 teaspoons orange-flavoured liqueur
- 440 g (14 oz) can apricot halves, drained and sliced
- 12 strawberries, halved or sliced
- 125 g (4 oz) seedless green or black grapes, halved
- 2 peaches, sliced
- 2 kiwifruit, sliced

makes 18

1 Preheat oven to 190°C (375°F, gas mark 5). In a food processor, place plain flour and icing sugar and process to combine. Add butter and process until resembles fine breadcrumbs. With machine running, add egg yolks and water and process to form a rough dough. Turn dough onto a lightly floured surface and knead until smooth. Wrap dough in plastic wrap. Refrigerate for 20 minutes.

2 Roll out dough to 3 mm (1/10-in.) thick. Using an 8 cm (3-in.) pastry cutter, cut out 18 rounds. Place rounds in lightly greased patty pans (tartlet tins). Prick base and sides of pastry with a fork and bake for 10 minutes or until golden. Cool on a wire rack.

3 In a bowl, place sugar, cornflour, eggs and egg yolk and whisk until smooth and thick. Heat milk and cream in a small pan over a medium heat, then gradually whisk in egg mixture. Reduce heat to low and cook, stirring constantly, until mixtures boils and thickens. Remove from heat, stir in liqueur. Cover and set aside to cool.

4 To assemble: In a bowl, place gelatine and boiling water and stir until gelatine dissolves. Stir in jam and 2 teaspoons liqueur and set aside until glaze cools and begins to thicken. Spoon custard cream filling into pastry shells, then decorate with fruit and brush tops with gelatine mixture. Chill until firm.

Nutritional value per serve Fat: 4.7 g Carbohydrate: 30 g Protein: 3.7 g

Orange and blueberry upside-down cakes

Preparation time 20 minutes Cooking time 30 minutes

Ingredients

Orange and blueberry topping

- 2 small oranges, peeled
- 155 g (5 oz) fresh or frozen blueberries
- 1 tablespoon cornflour
- 1 tablespoon brown sugar
- 2 tablespoons sherry or brandy

Almond cakes

- 115 g (4 oz) raw unsalted almonds, roasted and ground to a meal
- 90 g (3 oz) plain flour
- 1 teaspoon baking powder
- 4 egg whites
- 125 g (4 oz) sugar
- 2 egg yolks
- 1 teaspoon vanilla essence

Orange custard (optional)

- 1 cup (250 g, 8 oz) low-fat custard
- 2 teaspoons orange blossom water, orange juice or orange-flavoured liqueur
- 2 teaspoons grated orange rind (zest)

makes 12

1 In a jug, place custard, orange blossom water and orange rind. Mix to combine. Cover and refrigerate until ready to use.

2 In a large saucepan, place oranges and water to cover. Bring to the boil. Reduce heat. Simmer for 10 minutes. Drain and set aside until cool enough to handle.

3 Preheat oven to 170°C (325°F, gas mark 3). Lightly spray or brush two non-stick 1-cup (250 ml, 8 fl oz) capacity muffin trays with unsaturated oil.

4 In a large bowl, place blueberries, cornflour, sugar and sherry. Toss to combine. Place an orange slice in the base of each muffin cup. Top with some of the blueberry mixture. Set aside.

5 Sift together ground almonds, flour and baking powder. In a large bowl, place egg whites and beat until soft peaks form. Gradually beat in sugar. Beat in egg yolks and vanilla essence. Continue beating until sugar dissolves.

6 Using a large spoon or spatula, fold in the flour mixture until just combined – do not over-mix. Spoon batter into muffin cups. Bake for 15–20 minutes or until cooked when tested with a skewer. Stand muffins in tins for 5–10 minutes. Turn onto a wire rack. Serve warm with orange custard, if desired.

2

4

Nutritional value per serve Fat: 4 g Carbohydrate: 16.4 g Protein: 6.8 g

Macadamia and coffee marzipan

Preparation time 20 minutes, plus overnight refrigeration

Ingredients

- 270 g (9 oz) ground unsalted macadamias
- 100 g (3½ oz) pure icing sugar
- 100 g (3½ oz) castor sugar
- 6 teaspoons egg white (about 1 egg white)
- 1 tablespoon instant coffee dissolved in 1 tablespoon hot water
- few drops vanilla essence
- confectioner's rice paper

makes 36

1 In a food processor, place ground macadamias, icing sugar and castor sugar. Process to combine. With machine running, slowly add egg white. Process until mixture just holds together.

2 Divide mixture in half and place in two bowls. Add coffee to one portion. Knead to combine. Add vanilla essence to the other portion. Knead to combine.

3 Line an 18 cm (7-in.) square shallow cake tin with rice paper. Press the coffee-flavoured mixture firmly into tin. Press vanilla-flavoured mixture on top. Cover lightly with greaseproof paper. Refrigerate overnight or until ready for use.

4 To serve, remove greaseproof paper. Cut into 3 cm (1-in.) squares or desired shapes.

Nutritional value per serve Fat: 26.5 g Carbohydrate: 22 g Protein: 4 g

Mango cake with nutmeg

Preparation time 15 minutes Cooking time 1 hour

Ingredients
160 g (5½ oz) unsalted, roasted macadamia nuts
3 large mangoes
255 g (8 oz) butter
250 g (8 oz) castor sugar
1 teaspoon vanilla essence
4 large eggs
250 g (8 oz) plain flour
1½ teaspoons baking powder
80 g (3 oz) roasted macadamia nuts, chopped
icing sugar
2 cups (500 ml, 16 fl oz) thickened cream
1 teaspoon nutmeg
1 mango, sliced, for serving
serves 6

1 Preheat the oven to 180°C (350°F, gas mark 4) and butter a 22 cm (8-in.) non-stick cake tin.

2 Crush 160 g (5⅓ oz) roasted macadamia nuts in a food processor and set aside. Peel the mangoes and dice the flesh, saving as much juice as possible. Reserve about ½ cup mango dices and purée the remainder (about 1 cup of mango purée).

3 Cream the softened butter and vanilla essence with ½ cup (125 g, 4 oz) sugar and beat until thick and pale. Add remaining sugar and beat until all sugar has been added. Add the eggs, one at a time, and beat well after each addition.

4 In a separate bowl, mix the crushed nuts, flour and baking powder together. Fold in the flour mixture, stirring well to combine. Add the mango purée and mix gently.

5 Spoon the batter into the tin. Sprinkle over chopped macadamia nuts and reserved diced mango and swirl through. Bake at 170°C (325°F, gas mark 3) for 1 hour, remove from the oven and cool in the tin. When cool, remove cake from the tin. Dredge with icing sugar. In a bowl, whip the cream and nutmeg together until the cream is thick and fragrant. Serve alongside the cake with some mango slices.

Nutritional value per serve Fat: 29.3 g Carbohydrate: 19 g Protein: 2.6 g

Rum and lime banana fritters

Preparation time 10 minutes, plus 30 minutes marinating Cooking time 7 minutes

Ingredients

- 4 bananas
- juice of 1 lime
- 2 teaspoons castor sugar
- 1 tablespoon dark rum
- oil for deep-frying

batter

- 100 g (3½ oz) self-raising flour
- pinch of salt
- 150 ml (5 fl oz) water
- 2 tablespoons sesame seeds

serves 4

1 Peel each banana and cut in half crossways, then slice lengthways to make quarters. Place the banana quarters, lime juice, sugar and rum in a deep, non-metallic dish and mix gently. Cover and set aside for 30 minutes to marinate.

2 Sift the flour and salt into a mixing bowl. Pour in 150 ml (5 fl oz) water and whisk to form a smooth, thick batter. Stir in the sesame seeds and set aside.

3 Heat 5 cm (2-in.) of oil in a wok or large frying pan until smoking hot. Coat the banana pieces thoroughly in the batter. Fry for 5 minutes or until golden brown. Turn over and cook for 2 minutes to brown the other side. Drain on kitchen towels.

Nutritional value per serve Fat: 11.1 g Carbohydrate: 15 g Protein: 6.9 g

Baked passionfruit custards

Preparation time 10 minutes Cooking time 40 minutes

Ingredients

- 4 large eggs, beaten
- 4 tablespoons castor sugar
- 150 ml (5 fl oz) coconut milk
- pinch of salt
- 2 passionfruits

serves 4

1 Preheat the oven to 180°C (350°F, gas mark 4). Whisk together the eggs, sugar, coconut milk and salt until smooth, then pour into 4 ramekins.

2 Halve 1 passionfruit, scoop out the pulp and seeds and divide between the 4 custard-filled ramekins. Place ramekins in a deep roasting tin.

3 Pour boiling water into the roasting tin to three-quarters of the way up the sides of the ramekins. Bake the custards for 40 minutes. Serve warm or cold with the pulp and seeds from the remaining passionfruit spooned over the top.

3

Nutritional value per serve Fat: 0.2 g Carbohydrate: 13 g Protein: 0.7 g

Oriental fruit salad

Preparation time 15 minutes, plus 20 minutes cooling and 30 minutes chilling

Cooking time 5 minutes

Ingredients
3 stalks lemongrass
60 g (2 oz) castor sugar
100 ml ($3\frac{1}{2}$ fl oz) water
1 small rock melon (cantaloupe)
1 mango
425 g (14 oz) can lychees, drained
fresh mint leaves to garnish

serves 4

1 Peel the outer layers from the lemongrass stalks and finely chop the lower white bulbous parts. In a pan, place the lemongrass, sugar and 100 ml ($3\frac{1}{2}$ fl oz) water. Simmer, stirring, for 5 minutes or until sugar dissolves, then bring to the boil. Remove from heat and leave to cool for 20 minutes. Refrigerate for 30 minutes.

2 Halve the melon and scrape out the seeds. Cut into wedges, remove skin and cut the flesh into small chunks. Slice off the two fat sides of the mango close to the stone. Cut a criss-cross pattern across the flesh, of each piece, then push the skin up to expose the cubes of flesh and cut them off. Place the melon, mango and lychees in serving bowls. Strain the lemongrass syrup and pour over the fruit. Decorate with mint.

Nutritional value per serve Fat: 13.3 g Carbohydrate: 28 g Protein: 9.6 g

Almond rice jelly

Preparation time 5 minutes Cooking time 10 minutes

Ingredients

- 90 g (3 oz) ground rice
- 170 g (5½ oz) ground almonds
- 60 g (2 oz) powdered gelatine
- 170 g (5½ oz) castor sugar
- 60 g (2 oz) dessicated coconut
- 1.2 litres (2 pints) boiling water
- few drops of almond essence (extract)
- 200 g (7 oz) can lychees
- 250 g (8 oz) strawberries

serves 6–8

1 Into a saucepan, place ground rice, almonds, gelatine, sugar and coconut and mix to combine. Add, while stirring, the boiling water. Bring to the boil and simmer, still stirring for 10 minutes until thick. Stir in almond essence.

2 Pour into a lightly-greased fluted mould, cool, cover and refrigerate.

3 Unmould the rice jelly onto a plate. Garnish with the lychees and the strawberries.

1

2

Nutritional value per serve Fat: 8.7 g Carbohydrate: 30 g Protein: 2.8 g

Caramelised rice pudding with apricots

Preparation time 10 minutes, plus 20 minutes cooling and 1 hour refrigeration
Cooking time 1 hour, 10 minutes

Ingredients

- 75 g (2½ oz) short-grain rice
- 200 g (7 oz) castor sugar
- 2 vanilla pods, 1 split in half lengthways
- 2 tablespoons unsalted butter
- 600 ml (1 pint) full-fat milk
- 145 ml (5 fl oz) thickened cream
- 2 strips lemon rind (zest)
- 250 g (8 oz) dried apricots
- 2 tablespoons lemon juice
- 1–2 tablespoons cointreau

serves 4

1 Into a saucepan, put the rice and cover with water. Boil for 5 minutes and drain. Return the rice to the saucepan with 45 g (1½ oz) sugar, 1 of the vanilla pods, butter and milk. Simmer for 45–60 minutes, stirring often, until thickened. Transfer to a bowl and cool for 20 minutes or until cold. Remove the vanilla pod and scrape the seeds into the rice. Discard the pod. Whisk the cream until it forms soft peaks, then fold into the rice.

2 Meanwhile, put 100 g (3½ oz) of the sugar into a saucepan with the lemon, remaining vanilla pod and 200 ml (7 fl oz) of water. Heat, stirring, until the sugar dissolves. Add the apricots and cook for 10–15 minutes until syrup has thickened. Stir in the lemon juice and liqueur, stand to cool for 5 minutes.

3 Divide the apricots and syrup between 4 ramekins. Top with the rice pudding and refrigerate for 1 hour. Preheat the grill to high. Sprinkle the puddings with the rest of the sugar. Grill for 1–2 minutes until the sugar caramelises. Remove and stand 5 minutes to cool before serving.

Nutritional value per serve Fat: 4.1 g Carbohydrate: 40 g Protein: 1.5 g

Risotto of caramelised apples and pears

Preparation time 10 minutes Cooking time 35 minutes

Ingredients

- 3 tablespoons butter
- 3 tablespoons sugar
- 2 tablespoons maple syrup
- 2 Golden Delicious apples, peeled, cored and sliced
- 1 brown pear, peeled, cored and sliced
- 1 teaspoon cinnamon
- 600 ml (1 pint) apple juice
- 300 ml (10 fl oz) water
- 1 tablespoon butter
- 400 g (13 oz) arborio rice
- 100 ml (3½ fl oz) white wine
- 4 tablespoons sour cream
- ½ teaspoon cinnamon
- 1 red apple, coarse grated and tossed with lemon juice

serves 4–6

1 In a non-stick frying pan, heat the butter, sugar and maple syrup. Boil about 3 minutes until syrupy. Add the sliced fruit and cinnamon, and toss. Simmer the fruit about 10–15 minutes until caramelised and golden. Set aside.

2 In a pan, combine apple juice and water and heat to simmering. In a saucepan, melt the butter, add the rice and stir to coat. Add the wine and simmer until the liquid is absorbed. Begin to add the simmering apple water, 1 cup (250 ml, 8 fl oz) at a time, stirring well after each addition and allowing the liquid to be absorbed before the next addition.

3 When half the apple water has been absorbed, add the caramelised apples and pears and stir well to distribute. Continue adding the apple water as before until it has all been absorbed.

4 Remove the pan from the heat and add half the sour cream. Stir well to distribute and allow to cool. Serve in individual bowls, garnished with a small dollop of sour cream, a sprinkling of cinnamon and some grated apple.

Nutritional value per serve Fat: 8.4 g Carbohydrate: 36 g Protein: 5.2 g

Classic blueberry muffins

Preparation time 15 minutes Cooking time 30 minutes

Ingredients

315 g (10 oz) self-raising flour

1 teaspoon baking powder

90 g (3 oz) sugar

2 eggs, lightly beaten

1 cup (250 ml, 8 fl oz) buttermilk or milk

4 tablespoons butter, melted

155 g (5 oz) blueberries

1 tablespoon finely grated orange rind (zest)

2 tablespoons coffee sugar crystals or raw sugar

extra butter for greasing

makes 6

1 Preheat oven to 200°C (400°F, gas mark 6). Into a large bowl, sift flour and baking powder. Add sugar and combine.

2 In a separate bowl, combine eggs, milk and butter. Add egg mixture, blueberries and orange rind to flour mixture and mix until just combined.

3 Spoon mixture into 6 greased 1-cup (250 ml, 8 fl oz) capacity muffin tins. Sprinkle with coffee sugar crystals or raw sugar and bake for 20–30 minutes or until muffins are cooked when tested with a skewer. Turn onto a wire rack to cool.

3

Nutritional value per serve Fat: 9.1 g Carbohydrate: 29 g Protein: 6 g

Spiced apple muffins

Preparation time 20 minutes Cooking time 20 minutes

Ingredients

- 200 g (7 oz) plain wholemeal flour
- 1 tablespoon baking powder
- 1 teaspoon ground mixed spice
- pinch of salt
- 4 tablespoons brown sugar
- 1 medium egg, beaten
- 220 ml (7½ fl oz) low-fat milk
- 4 tablespoons butter
- 1 cooking apple, peeled, cored and chopped

makes 9

1 Preheat oven to 200°C (400°F, gas mark 6). Line a muffin or deep bun tin with 9 muffin cases and set aside. In a large bowl, combine flour, baking powder, mixed spice and salt.

2 In another large bowl, combine sugar, egg, milk and melted butter. Gently fold in the flour mixture until just combined – do not over-handle. The mixture should be quite lumpy. Gently fold in apple.

3 Divide mixture between the muffin cases. Bake in the oven for 20 minutes or until cooked when tested with a skewer. Transfer to a wire rack to cool.

Nutritional value per serve Fat: 16.9 g Carbohydrate: 35 g Protein: 5.5 g

Lemon poppy seed muffins

Preparation time 20 minutes Cooking time 30 minutes

Ingredients

- 2 eggs, lightly beaten
- 1 cup (250 ml, 8 fl oz) sour cream
- ½ cup (125 ml, 4 fl oz) milk
- 4 tablespoons oil
- 4 tablespoons honey
- 3 tablespoons poppy seeds
- 1 tablespoon grated lemon rind (zest)
- 280 g (9 oz) self-raising flour, sifted
- butter for greasing

Lemon cream cheese icing

- 4 tablespoons cream cheese, softened
- 1 tablespoon lemon juice
- 125 g (4 oz) icing sugar

makes 6

1 Preheat oven to 180°C (350°F, gas mark 4). In a large bowl, combine eggs, sour cream, milk, oil, honey, poppy seeds and lemon rind.

2 Add flour to poppy seed mixture and mix until just combined.

3 Spoon mixture into 6 greased 1-cup (250 ml, 8 fl oz) capacity muffin tins and bake for 25–30 minutes or until muffins are cooked when tested with a skewer. Turn onto a wire rack to cool.

4 In a food processor, combine cream cheese, lemon juice and icing sugar until smooth. Top cooled muffins with icing.

1

4

Nutritional value per serve Fat: 19.4 g Carbohydrate: 40 g Protein: 6.7 g

Choc rough muffins

Preparation time 15 minutes Cooking time 35 minutes

Ingredients

- 125 g (4 oz) butter
- 1/2 cup (125 g, 4 oz) sugar
- 2 eggs, lightly beaten
- 250 g (8 oz) self-raising flour, sifted
- 4 tablespoons cocoa powder, sifted
- 175 g (5 1/2 oz) chocolate chips
- 45 g (1 1/2 oz) desiccated coconut
- 3/4 cup (185 ml, 6 fl oz) buttermilk or milk

makes 6

1 Preheat oven to 180°C (350°F, gas mark 4). In a large bowl, place butter and sugar and beat until light and fluffy. Gradually beat in eggs.

2 In a separate bowl, combine flour and cocoa powder. Add flour mixture, chocolate chips, coconut and milk to butter mixture and mix until just combined.

3 Spoon mixture into 6 greased 1-cup (250 ml, 8 fl oz) capacity muffin tins and bake for 35 minutes or until muffins are cooked when tested with a skewer. Turn onto a wire rack to cool.

Nutritional value per serve Fat: 16.2 g Carbohydrate: 40 g Protein: 4 g

Sticky date muffins

Preparation time 20 minutes Cooking time 40 minutes

Ingredients
250 g (8 oz) self-raising flour
1 teaspoon bicarbonate of soda
1 teaspoon ground cinnamon
4 tablespoons brown sugar
90 g (3 oz) butter
125 g (4 oz) pitted dates, chopped
1 egg, lightly beaten
1 cup (250 ml, 8 fl oz) buttermilk or milk
Brandy sauce
100 g (3½ oz) butter
3 tablespoons brown sugar
1 tablespoon golden syrup
1 tablespoon brandy
makes 6

1 Preheat oven to 190°C (375°F, gas mark 5). Into a large bowl, sift flour, bicarbonate of soda and cinnamon. Set aside.

2 Place 4 tablespoons sugar, 90 g (3 oz) butter and dates in a small pan and heat over a low heat, stirring constantly until butter melts. Pour date mixture into dry ingredients, add egg and milk. Mix until just combined.

3 Spoon mixture into 6 greased 1-cup (250 ml, 8 fl oz) capacity muffin tins and bake for 30 minutes until muffins are cooked when tested with a skewer. Turn onto a wire rack.

4 Place remaining butter and sugar, golden syrup and brandy in a small pan and heat over a low heat, stirring constantly, until sugar dissolves. Bring to the boil, reduce heat and simmer for 3 minutes until sauce is thick and syrupy. Serve with warm muffins.

Nutritional value per serve Fat: 23.9 g Carbohydrate: 36 g Protein: 5.8 g

Mini chocolate muffins with mocha sauce

Preparation time 20 minutes Cooking time 20 minutes

Ingredients

60 g (2 oz) unsalted butter, diced, plus extra for greasing

60 g (2 oz) plain cooking chocolate, roughly chopped

2 medium eggs

100 g (3½ oz) castor sugar

100 g (3½ oz) self-raising flour

30 g (1 oz) cocoa powder, sifted, plus extra for dusting

Mocha sauce

150 g (5 oz) plain chocolate, roughly chopped

90 mL (3 fl oz) espresso or other strong, good quality coffee

155 mL (5 oz) thickened cream

makes 12

1 Preheat oven to 180ºC (350ºF, gas mark 4). Melt chocolate and butter in a bowl set over a pan of simmering water. In a large bowl, place the eggs, sugar, flour and cocoa powder. Beat for 1 minute then fold in melted chocolate and butter.

2 Spoon batter into 12 greased ½-cup (125 ml, 4 fl oz) capacity muffin tins. Bake for 15 minutes or until muffins are cooked when tested with a skewer. Turn onto wire racks to cool.

3 Place the chocolate, coffee and 4 tablespoons of the cream into a small pan and heat gently. Simmer for 1–2 minutes, until sauce has thickened slightly. Keep warm.

4 Allow muffins to cool on a wire rack for 5 minutes. Whisk remaining cream until thickened, spoon over the muffins along with the mocha sauce. Serve dusted with cocoa powder.

Nutritional value per serve Fat: 5.7 g Carbohydrate: 30 g Protein: 5.6 g

Banana and pineapple muffins

Preparation time 20 minutes Cooking time 15 minutes

Ingredients
185 g (6 oz) wholemeal self-raising flour
1 teaspoon baking powder
1 teaspoon mixed spice
4 tablespoons brown sugar
45 g (1½ oz) oat bran
1 small banana, mashed
150 g (5 oz) can crushed pineapple, drained
3 egg whites, lightly beaten
2 tablespoons vegetable oil
½ cup (125 ml, 4 fl oz) pineapple juice
makes 12

1 Preheat oven to 200°C (400°F, gas mark 6). Into a large bowl, sift flour, baking powder and spice. Add sugar and oat bran and mix to combine.

2 Make a well in the centre of the flour mixture. In a separate bowl, combine banana, pineapple, egg whites, oil and juice. Stir into flour mixture and mix until just combined.

3 Spoon mixture into lightly greased ½-cup (125 ml, 4 fl oz) capacity muffin tins. Bake for 12–15 minutes or until muffins are cooked when tested with a skewer. Turn onto a wire rack to cool.

1

2

Nutritional value per serve Fat: 8.4 g Carbohydrate: 32 g Protein: 4.8 g

Carrot ginger muffins

Preparation time 20 minutes Cooking time 18 minutes

Ingredients
250 g (8 oz) unbleached plain flour
1 tablespoon baking powder
1 teaspoon bicarbonate of soda
½ teaspoon salt
½ teaspoon ground nutmeg
½ teaspoon ground cinnamon
2 teaspoons freshly grated ginger
½ cup (125 ml, 4 fl oz) yoghurt or buttermilk
4 tablespoons vegetable oil
4 tablespoons maple syrup
4 tablespoons honey
3 eggs
310 g (10 oz) carrot, grated
makes 12

1 Preheat oven to 200°C (400°F, gas mark 6). In a large bowl combine flour, baking powder, bicarbonate of soda, salt, nutmeg and cinnamon.

2 In a separate bowl, combine ginger, yoghurt, oil, maple syrup, honey and eggs. Add egg mixture to flour mixture and mix to combine. Stir in carrots.

3 Spoon mixture into greased ½-cup (125 ml, 4 fl oz) capacity muffin tins. Bake for 15–18 minutes or until muffins are cooked when tested with a skewer. Serve warm.

Nutritional value per serve Fat: 12.2 g Carbohydrate: 32 g Protein: 6.1 g

Fresh strawberry scones

Preparation time 15 minutes Cooking time 10 minutes

Ingredients
225 g (7½ oz) self-raising wholemeal flour
1 teaspoon baking powder
pinch of salt
4 tablespoons butter
2 tablespoons castor sugar
100 g (3½ oz) fresh strawberries, chopped
½ cup (125 ml, 4 fl oz) low-fat milk
extra milk for glazing

makes 12

1 Preheat oven to 220°C (425°F, gas mark 7). In a large bowl, place flour, baking powder and salt and mix to combine. Lightly rub in the butter with fingertips until the mixture resembles breadcrumbs.

2 Add sugar, strawberries and enough milk to form a soft dough. Turn the dough out onto a floured surface, knead lightly, then carefully roll to a thickness of 2 cm (1-in.).

3 Cut out 12 rounds, using a 5-cm (2-in.) pastry cutter, and place side by side on a baking sheet. Brush with milk to glaze. Bake for 8–10 minutes, until risen and golden brown. Transfer to a wire rack to cool.

Nutritional value per serve Fat: 10.9 g Carbohydrate: 34 g Protein: 5.7 g

Pumpkin scones

Preparation time 15 minutes Cooking time 20 minutes

Ingredients
4 tablespoons butter
2 tablespoons castor sugar
125 g (4 oz) pumpkin, cooked and mashed
1/4 teaspoon nutmeg
1 egg
1/2 cup (125 ml, 4 fl oz) milk
285 g (9 oz) self-raising flour, sifted
makes 12

1 Preheat oven to 210°C (415°F, gas mark 6–7). In a large bowl, cream butter and sugar until well combined. Add pumpkin and nutmeg and mix well. Add egg, then gradually add milk. Stir in sifted flour and gently mix to a soft dough.

2 Turn dough onto a floured surface and knead lightly, then carefully roll to a thickness of 2½ cm (1-in.). Cut out 12 rounds using a 5 cm (2-in.) pastry cutter.

3 Place onto a greased baking sheet and brush with milk to glaze. Bake for 15–20 minutes until risen and golden brown. Transfer to a wire rack to cool. Serve with butter.

Nutritional value per serve Fat: 13.2 g Carbohydrate: 33 g Protein: 5 g

Blueberry pecan loaf

Preparation time 25 minutes Cooking time 65 minutes

Ingredients

- 250 g (8 oz) unbleached plain flour
- 2 teaspoon baking powder
- 1/2 teaspoon salt
- 1/4 teaspoon bicarbonate of soda
- 1/4 teaspoon ground nutmeg
- 125 g (4 oz) sugar
- 60 g (2 oz) pecans, chopped
- 2 eggs
- 4 tablespoons milk
- 1/2 cup (125 ml, 4 fl oz) orange juice
- 2 teaspoons grated orange rind (zest)
- 90 g (3 oz) butter, melted
- 155 g (5 oz) blueberries

makes 1

1 Preheat oven to 180°C (350°F, gas mark 4). In a large bowl combine flour, baking powder, salt, bicarbonate of soda, nutmeg and sugar. Mix in pecans. Make a well in the centre.

2 In a medium bowl, beat eggs with milk, orange juice and rind. Fold in melted butter. Add egg mixture to flour mixture, mixing until just combined. Gently fold in blueberries.

3 Pour batter into a well-greased 20 x 10 cm (8 x 4-in.) loaf tin. Bake for 55–65 minutes until loaf is golden and risen. Cool in pan for 10 minutes. Turn onto a wire rack to cool.

1

2

Nutritional value per serve Fat: 17.1 g Carbohydrate: 41 g Protein: 6.5 g

Chocolate chip orange bread

Preparation time 20 minutes Cooking time 60 minutes

Ingredients
250 g (8 oz) unbleached plain flour
2 teaspoons baking powder
1/2 teaspoon salt
1/4 teaspoon bicarbonate of soda
125 g (4 oz) sugar
60 g (2 oz) chopped walnuts
150 g (5 oz) chocolate chips
2 eggs
4 tablespoons milk
1/2 cup (125 ml, 4 fl oz) orange juice
2 teaspoons grated orange rind (zest)
1 teaspoon vanilla extract
90 g (3 oz) butter, melted
makes 1

1 Preheat oven to 180°C (350°F, gas mark 4). In a large bowl, combine flour, baking powder, salt, bicarbonate of soda and sugar. Add walnuts and 3/4 cup of the chocolate chips, mix to combine. Make a well in the centre.

2 In a medium bowl, beat eggs with milk, orange juice, orange rind and vanilla. Fold in butter. Pour egg mixture into flour mixture, mixing until just combined.

3 Pour batter into a well-greased 20 x 10 cm (8 x 4-in.) loaf tin. Sprinkle evenly with remaining chocolate chips. Bake for 55–60 minutes until golden and risen. Cool in tin for 10 minutes. Turn onto a wire rack to cool.

index

a

almond 109
almond rice jelly 158
apricot
  caramelised rice pudding with apricots 159
  easy apricot and mango chicken loaf 110
  spiced apricot meatballs 22
apricot canapés 10
apricot chicken pilaf 114
apple
  parsnip and apple soup with garlic croutons 3
  risotto of caramelised apples and pears 160
  spiced apple muffins 162
asian gingered coleslaw 61
asparagus
  herbed rice noodles with asparagus and peanuts 45
  tagliatelle with asparagus and prosciutto 34
asparagus and baby green beans with hazelnut dressing 57
asparagus, ricotta and herb frittata 90

b

bake 87
baked passionfruit custards 156
baked ricotta mushrooms 98
balinese chicken satay 24
banana 155
banana and pineapple muffins 167
basil 96
bean, lentil and eggplant moussaka 88
bean
  asparagus and baby green beans with hazelnut dressing 57
  eggplant with bean and basil 96
  lamb shanks with broad beans, olives and risoni 144
  three bean rice salad 66
  warm butter bean and prosciutto salad with rocket 64
bean sprouts 46
beef
  honey beef with pineapple salsa 135
  indonesian beef curry 139
  korean marinated beef strips 137
  thai beef salad with chilli lime dressing 134
  warm steak salad with pawpaw and spanish onion 141
beef with black been sauce 44
beetroot
  roasted beetroot, orange and fennel salad 60
  grilled brie with beetroot salad 55
black bean 44
blueberry
  classic blueberry muffins 161
  orange and blueberry upside down cakes 152
blueberry pecan loaf 171
blue cheese and walnut damper 73
bok choy 83
bread
  chocolate chip orange bread 172
  sun-dried tomato and provolone quick bread 74
breadcrumbs 120
brie
  grilled brie with beetroot salad 55
  tomato, mustard and brie tart 86
broccoli
  chicken and broccoli lasagne 31
  seafood and broccoli risotto 38
broccoli soufflés and olive purée 93
bruschetta 54
butter bean 64

c

cabbage and chinese noodle salad 65
cajun barbecue corn 91
cake
  mango cake with nutmeg 154
  orange and blueberry upside-down cakes 152
  thai fish cakes with peanut dipping sauce 21
calamari rings 26

canapés 10
cannelloni 121
capsicum
  gnocchi with pork and capsicums 130
  penne with capsicum and mascarpone 69
  roasted capsicum and tomato soup 77
caramelised rice pudding with apricots 159
carrot ginger muffins 168
char-grilled tuna with peach salsa 119
cheese
  asparagus, ricotta and herb frittata 90
  baked ricotta mushrooms 98
  blue cheese and walnut damper 73
  cheesy baked rice 42
  grilled brie with beetroot salad 55
  meat ravioli with cream and parmesan 32
  mixed vegetable cheese bake 87
  oven-baked parmesan chicken 106
  penne with capsicum and mascarpone 69
  potato fetta fritters 58
  ricotta herb dip with garlic toasts 7
  risotto with baby spinach and gorgonzola 67
  spinach and nutmeg soup with cheese toasts 5
  spinach, fish and ricotta cannelloni 121
  sun-dried tomato and provolone quick bread 74
  tomato, mustard and brie tart 86
  vine tomatoes and goat's cheese bruschetta 54
  wilted rocket cheese salad 85
chicken
  apricot chicken pilaf 114
  balinese chicken satay 24
  curried chicken rolls 15
  easy apricot and mango chicken loaf 110
  fruited chicken pasta salad 36
  hawaiian poached chicken 105
  hot chicken ball salad with fruity dressing 112
  lime-glazed chicken wings 25
  linguine with chicken and mushrooms 108
  moroccan lemon chicken shish kebabs 23
  mustard and honey chicken drumsticks with mustard cream sauce 107
  oven-baked parmesan chicken 106
  penne with chicken sauce 35
  vindaloo chicken nuggets 16
  warm thai chicken salad 111
chicken and broccoli lasagne 31
chicken and leek flan with almond topping 109
chicken and leek soup with herb dumplings 102
chicken and mushroom linguine 108
chicken and prune roll 103
chicken laksa 101
chicken party sticks 18
chicken rogan josh 104
chicken waldorf 113
chilli 95
chilli fried rice 43
chilli lime dressing 134
chinese-style steamed grey mullet 122
chocolate
  choc rough muffins 164
  mini chocolate muffins with mocha sauce 166
  chocolate chip orange bread 172
classic blueberry muffins 161
coconut
  goan-style fish and coconut curry 47
  spring vegetables in spiced coconut curry 81
coconut prawns and scallops 118
coffee 153
coleslaw 61
coriander 51
corn 91
couscous salad with seafood and fresh mint 124
cream
  meat ravioli with cream and parmesan 32
  potato sour cream muffins 71
croissant 19
curried chicken rolls 15
curry
  goan-style fish and coconut curry 47
  indonesian beef curry 139
  keema curry 135
  spring vegetables in spiced coconut curry 81
custard 156

d

dahl 51
damper 73
date 165
dauphinoise 92
dressing
  fruity 112
  chilli lime 134
dumpling 102

e

easy apricot and mango chicken loaf 110
eggplant with bean with basil 96

f

fetta, potato fetta fritters 58
fennel 60
fire and spice risotto 40

fish
- char-grilled tuna with peach salsa 119
- chinese-style steamed grey mullet 122
- goan-style fish and coconut curry 47
- home-smoked trout 123
- lime fish with noodles 116
- oriental-style salmon fillets 117
- spinach, fish and ricotta cannelloni 121
- thai fish cakes with peanut dipping sauce 21

flan 109
fragrant pilaf 68
fresh herb and oat scones 72
fresh strawberry scones 169
frittata
- asparagus, ricotta and herb frittata 90
- roast pumpkin, potato and rosemary frittatas 20

fritter
- potato fetta fritters 58
- rum and lime banana fritters 155

fruit 156
fruit tartlets 151
fruited chicken pasta salad 36

g

garlic
- lamb with lemon and garlic 144
- parsnip and apple soup with garlic croutons 3
- ricotta herb dip with garlic toasts 7

ginger
- asian gingered coleslaw 61
- carrot ginger muffins 168
- split lentil dhal with ginger and coriander 51

gingered thai rice salad 37
glazed pork spare ribs 132
gnocchi with pork and capsicums 130
goan-style fish and coconut curry 47
gorgonzola 67
greek shish kebabs 146
green vegetable stir-fry with sesame seeds 82
grilled brie with beetroot salad 55

h

hawaiian poached chicken 105
hazelnut 57
herb
- asparagus, ricotta and herb frittata 90
- chicken and leek soup with herb dumplings 102
- fresh herb and oat scones 72
- ricotta herb dip with garlic toasts 7
- warm caramelised onion and herbed potato salad 63

herbed and spiced pork loin 133
herbed rice noodles with asparagus and peanuts 45
home-smoked trout 123
honey
- lamb with honeyed onions 147
- mustard and honey chicken drumsticks with mustard cream sauce 107

honey beef with pineapple salsa 136

i

indian meatballs in tomato sauce 140
indian-spiced potato and onion soup 79
indonesian beef curry 139

j

japanese prawn and vegetable tempura 6
jelly 158

k

kebab
- greek shish kebabs 144
- moroccan lemon chicken shish kebabs 23
- roman kebabs 53

keema curry 135
korean marinated beef strips 139

l

laksa 101
lamb fillets with salsa pilaf 142
lamb shanks with broad beans, olives and risoni 144
lamb with honeyed onions 147
lamb with lemon and garlic 145
lamb ragoût 143
lasagne
- chicken and broccoli 31
- vegetarian lasagne 97

leek
- chicken and leek flan with almond topping 109
- chicken and leek soup with herb dumplings 102
- linguine with leeks and mushrooms 89

lemon
- lamb with lemon and garlic 145
- moroccan lemon chicken shish kebabs 23

lemongrass pork skewers 129
lemon poppy seed muffins 163
lentil
  bean, lentil and eggplant moussaka 88
  spicy lentil soup 4
  split lentil dhal with ginger and coriander 51
lime
  chilli lime dressing 134
  lime fish with noodles 116
  rum and lime banana fritters 155
lime-glazed chicken wings 25
linguine with chicken and mushrooms 108
linguine with leeks and mushrooms 89
loaf 171

m

macadamia and coffee marzipan 153
macaroni with lamb ragoût 43
mango 110
mango cake with nutmeg 154
marzipan 153
mascarpone 69
meat ravioli with cream and parmesan 32
meatball
  indian meatballs in tomato sauce 140
  middle eastern spinach and meatball soup 127
  spiced apricot meatballs 22
minestrone 29
mini chocolate muffins with mocha sauce 166
mini pizzas 12
mini savoury croissants 19
mint 124
mixed vegetable cheese bake 87
moroccan lemon chicken shish kebabs 23
moussaka 88
muffins
  banana and pineapple 167
  carrot ginger muffins 168
  choc rough 164
  classic blueberry 161
  lemon poppy seed muffins 163
  mini chocolate muffins with mocha sauce 166
  potato sour cream muffins 71
  spiced apple muffins 162
  sticky date muffins 165
mullet 122
mushroom
  baked ricotta mushrooms 98
  chicken and mushroom linguine 108
  linguine with leeks and mushrooms 89
  mushrooms in wine 94
mustard
  mustard and honey chicken drumsticks with mustard cream sauce 107
  tomato, mustard and brie tart 86

n

nasi goring 39
noodle
cabbage and chinese noodle salad 65
  herbed rice noodles with asparagus and peanuts 45
  lime fish with noodles 116
  stir-fry pork with bean sprouts and noodles 46
nugget 16
nutmeg
  mango cake with nutmeg 154
  spinach and nutmeg soup with cheese toasts 5

o

oats 72
olive 144
olive purée 93
onion
  indian spiced potato and onion soup 79
  lamb with honeyed onions 144
  potato and onion dauphinoise 92
  red onion and chilli tarts 95
  warm caramelised onion and herbed potato salad 63
  warm steak salad with pawpaw and spanish onion 141
orange
  choc chip orange bread 172
  pan-fried pork steaks with orange and sage 131
  roasted beetroot, orange and fennel salad 60
  orange and blueberry upside-down cakes 152
oriental fruit salad 157
oriental-style salmon fillets 117
oven-baked parmesan chicken 106

p

pad thai with pork and prawns 48
pan-fried pork steaks with orange and sage 131
parmesan
  oven-baked parmesan chicken 106
  meat ravioli with cream and parmesan 32
parsnip and apple soup with garlic croutons 3
passionfruit 156

pasta
  chicken and mushroom linguine 108
  fruited chicken pasta salad 36
  gnocchi with pork and capsicums 130
  linguine with leeks and mushrooms 89
  pasta primavera 30
  penne with capsicum and mascarpone 69
  penne with chicken sauce 35
  spaghettini and scallops with breadcrumbs 120
  spinach, fish and ricotta cannelloni 121
  vegetarian lasagne 97
pawpaw 141
peanut dipping sauce 21
peanut
  herbed rice noodles with asparagus and peanuts 43
  sweet potato and peanut salad 70
pear 140
pecan 171
peach
  veal with peach melts 148
  peach salsa 119
penne with capsicum and mascarpone 69
penne with chicken sauce 35
persian-style pilaf 41
pesto
  pesto potato wedges 59
  spring onion pesto 78
  thick minestrone with pesto 29
pilaf
  apricot chicken pilaf 114
  fragrant pilaf 68
  lamb fillets with salsa pilaf 142
  persian-style pilaf 41
pineapple
  banana and pineapple muffins 167
  honey beef with pineapple salsa 136
pizza 12
polenta 52
poppy seed 163
pork
  glazed pork spare ribs 132
  gnocchi with pork and capsicums 130
  herbed and spiced pork loin 133
  lemongrass pork skewers 129
  pad thai with pork and prawns 48
  pan-fried pork steaks with orange and sage 131
  pork in walnut sauce 128
  stir-fry pork with bean sprouts and noodles 46
potato
  indian spiced potato and onion soup 70
  pesto potato wedges 59
  roast pumpkin, potato and rosemary frittatas 20
  warm caramelised onion and herbed potato salad 63
potato and onion dauphinoise 92
potato cakes with smoked salmon 8
potato fetta fritters 59
potato sour cream muffins 71
prawn
  coconut prawns and scallops 118
  japanese prawn and vegetable tempura 6
  pad thai with pork and prawns 48
  provençal-style soup with spring onion pesto 78
prosciutto
  prune and prosciutto rolls 11
  tagliatelle with asparagus and prosciutto 34
  warm butter bean and prosciutto salad with rocket 64
prune
  prune and prosciutto rolls 11
  chicken and prune roll 103
pudding 159
puff 17
pumpkin 20
pumpkin scones 170
purée
  sweet potato purée 56
  broccoli soufflés with olive purée 93

r

ravioli 32
red onion and chilli tarts 95
rice
  almond rice jelly 158
  cheesy basked rice 42
  chilli fried rice 43
  gingered thai rice salad 37
  nasi goring 39
  herbed rice noodles with asparagus and peanuts 45
  caramelised rice pudding with apricots 159
  three bean rice salad 66
ricotta
  asparagus, ricotta and herb frittata 90
  baked ricotta mushrooms 98
  ricotta herb dip with garlic toasts 7
  spinach, fish and ricotta cannelloni 121
risoni 144
risotto
  fire and spice risotto 40
  risotto of caramelised apples and pears 160
  risotto with baby spinach and gorgonzola 67
  seafood and broccoli risotto 38
roast pumpkin, potato and rosemary frittatas 20

roasted beetroot, orange and fennel salad 60
roasted capsicum and tomato soup 77
roasted vegetable salad 62
rocket
  wilted rocket cheese salad 85
  warm butter bean and prosciutto salad with rocket 64
roman kebabs 53
rolls
  chicken and prune roll 103
  curried chicken rolls 15
  prune and prosciutto rolls 11
  spring rolls 14
rosemary 20
rum and lime banana fritters 155

S

salad
  cabbage and Chinese noodle salad 65
  chicken waldof 113
  couscous salad with seafood and fresh mint 124
  fruited chicken pasta salad 36
  gingered thai rice salad 37
  grilled brie with beetroot salad 55
  hot chicken ball salad with fruity dressing 112
  oriental fruit salad 157
  roasted beetroot, orange and fennel salad 60
  roasted vegetable salad 62
  sweet potato and peanut salad 70
  thai beef salad with chilli lime dressing 134
  three bean rice salad 66
  warm butter bean and prosciutto salad with rocket 54
  warm caramelised onion and herbed potato salad 63
  warm spinach salad with walnuts 84
  warm steak salad with pawpaw and spanish onion 141
  warm thai chicken salad 111
  wilted rocket cheese salad 85
sage 131
salami stacks 9
salmon
  potato cakes with smoked salmon 8
  oriental-style salmon fillets 117
  smoked salmon soufflés 115
salsa
  peach 119
  pineapple 136
  chunky
samosa 13
satay 24
sauce
  black bean 44
  chicken 35
  mocha 166
  mustard cream 107
  peanut 21
  tomato 140
  walnut 128
scallop
  coconut prawns and scallops 118
  scallop puffs 17
  spaghettini and scallops with breadcrumbs 120
scone
  fresh herb and oat 72
  fresh strawberry 169
  pumpkin 170
seafood
  couscous salad with seafood and fresh mint 124
  seafood and broccoli risotto 38
  potato cakes with smoked salmon 8
  smoked salmon soufflés 115
  spaghettini and scallops with breadcrumbs 120
  spicy deep-fried calamari rings 26
sesame seed 82
shish kebab 23
slice 52
soufflé
  broccoli soufflés and olive purée 93
  smoked salmon soufflés 115
soup
  chicken and leek soup with herb dumplings 102
  indian spiced potato and onion soup 70
  middle eastern spinach and meatball soup 127
  parsnip and apple soup with garlic croutons 3
  provençal-style soup with spring onion pesto 78
  roasted capsicum and tomato soup 77
  spicy lentil soup 4
  spinach and nutmeg soup with cheese toasts 5
  thick minestrone with pesto 29
sour cream 71
spaghetti carbonara 33
spaghettini and scallops with breadcrumbs 120
spare rib 132
spiced apple muffins 162
spiced apricot meatballs 22
spicy deep-fried calamari rings 26
spicy lentil soup 4
spinach
  middle eastern spinach and meatball soup 127
  risotto with baby spinach and gorgonzola 67
  spinach and nutmeg soup with cheese toasts 5
  spinach, fish and ricotta cannelloni 121
  warm spinach salad with walnuts 84
split lentil dhal with ginger and coriander 51

spring roll 14
spring vegetables in spiced coconut curry 81
steak au poivre 138
sticky date muffins 165
stir-fry
  green vegetable stir-fry with sesame seeds 82
  stir-fry pork with bean sprouts and noodles 46
strawberry 169
sun-dried tomato and provolone quick bread 74
sweet potato and peanut salad 70
sweet potato purée 56

t

tagliatelle with asparagus and prosciutto 34
thai
  gingered thai rice salad 37
  warm thai chicken salad 111
  thai beef salad with chilli lime dressing 134
  thai fish cakes with peanut dipping sauce 21
tart
  red onion and chilli tarts 95
  fruit tartlets 151
  tomato, mustard and brie tart 86
tempura 6
thick minestrone with pesto 29
three bean rice salad 66
tofu and bok choy 83
tomato
  sun-dried tomato and provolone quick bread 74
  roasted capsicum and tomato soup 77
  vine tomatoes and goat's cheese bruschetta 54
  tomato, mustard and brie tart 86
  tomatoes yemistes 80
trout 123
tuna 119

v

veal and peach melts 148
vegetable saffron samosas 13
vegetarian lasagne 97
vietnamese spring rolls 14
vindaloo chicken nuggets 16
vine tomatoes and goat's cheese bruschetta 54

w

walnut
  blue cheese and walnut damper 73
  pork in walnut sauce 128
  warm spinach salad with walnuts 84
waldof salad 113
warm caramelised onion and herbed potato salad 63
warm butter bean and prosciutto salad with rocket 54
warm spinach salad with walnuts 84
warm steak salad with pawpaw and spanish onion 141
warm thai chicken salad 111
wedges 59
wilted rocket cheese salad 85
wine 94

z

zucchini polenta slices 52